Selected Poems 1933–1993

Selected Poems
1933–1993

Gavin Ewart

HUTCHINSON
London

© in this collection the Estate of Gavin Ewart, 1996

The right of Gavin Ewart to be identified as the Author of this work has
been asserted by Gavin Ewart in accordance with the Copyright, Designs and
Patents Act 1988

1 3 5 7 9 10 8 6 4 2

This edition first published in 1996 by Hutchinson

The poems in this book are taken from earlier collections, *The Collected Ewart:
Poems 1933–1980*, *Collected Poems 1980–1990* and *85 Poems*.

Random House (UK) Limited
20 Vauxhall Bridge Road, London SW1V 2SA

Random House Australia (Pty) Limited
20 Alfred Street, Milsons Point, Sydney,
New South Wales 2061, Australia

Random House New Zealand Limited
18 Poland Road, Glenfield, Auckland 10, New Zealand

Random House South Africa (Pty) Limited
Box 2263, Rosebank 2121, South Africa

A CIP record for this book is available from the British Library

Papers used by Random House UK Limited are natural, recyclable products
made from wood grown in sustainable forests. The manufacturing processes
conform to the environmental regulations of the country of origin.

ISBN 009 179176 6

Typeset in Bembo by Palimpsest Book Production Limited,
Polmont, Stirlingshire
Printed and bound in Great Britain by Mackays of Chatham PLC

The Song

I am a free ranging hen
and God put me on this earth
to pick up the crumbs of intelligence
I need for my artwork,
the old how, the variant where, the new when.

I am a Gauloise (blue)
for many years since my birth
I have been jumbling the words into elegance,
part pleasure, part work,
and I have been smoked by the many, bought by the few.

I am a sandwich fresh cut,
eat me aurally, near the bone
and juicy the ham was, desiccated
the pub clock will make it –
catch me by the vanishing rabbit's quick scut.

I am a bottle of wine,
the wrath in my grapes homegrown,
drink me; those who hesitated
were never able to take it.
Slup me rough and homely and I'll taste fine.

Contents

On the Author's Photograph

Yes, apprehensive eye,
We know, averted head.
I remember what I
Have done, have said.

Sleek head, you seal,
Shy pupil, still at school,
I know the pain you feel,
The pain of the fool.

Audenesque for an Initiation

Don't forget the things we taught you by the broken
    water-wheel,
Don't forget the middle-classes fight much harder going
    downhill,

Don't forget that new proscriptions are being posted now
    and then,
Dr Johnson, Dr Leavis and the other Grand Old Men –

Although they've very often told us that they try to do
    their best,
Are they up to the Full Fruit Standard, would they pass the
    Spelling Test?

– Because we've got our eyes to keyholes, we know everything
    they've done,
Lecturing on minor poets. 'Literature is quite good fun.'

And if you should try to fool us, imitate them, do the same,
We'll refuse your dummy bullets, we've had time to take
    our aim.

We've been drinking stagnant water for some twenty years
    or more
While the politicians slowly planned a bigger reservoir.

But we've dammed a different river, the water-wheel is
    going again.
Now we've stopped designing sweaters and we've started in
    to train.

We've given up the Georgian poets, teaching dance bands how
    to croon,
Bicycling in coloured goggles underneath a pallid moon.

We've destroyed the rotting signposts, made holes in all the
    pleasure boats;
We'll pull down ancestral castles when we've time to swim
    the moats.

When we've practised we shall beat you with our Third or
    Fourth Fifteen,
In spite of Royalists on the touchline. 'Oh, well played, Sir!'
    'Keep it clean!'

Our backs are fast as motor-cycles, all our forwards twenty-stone.
Each of them can score unaided, running strongly on his own.

Every minute scouts give signals, come reporting what
    they've seen.
'Captain Ferguson is putting.' 'Undermine the eighteenth green.'

Before next month we'll storm the clubhouse. Messages are
    coming through:
'Darwin, doing crossword puzzles, tries to find the missing clue.'

The *Times* Third Leaders are decoded, pigeon-holed for
    future use;
Tennyson has been convicted of incessant self-abuse.

We've been sending notes to Priestley, orange pips to J. C.
    Squire –

'Don't defend the trench you're holding.' 'Now the fat is in
  the fire.'

We've got control of all the railways and the perfume factories,
We're supercharged and have connection with the strongest
  batteries.

So if you feel like playing truant, remember that the game is up
Or you'll find that quite politely you've been sold a nasty pup.

Public School

A surname in this place
Is fitting. Keeps reserved
Emotional platoons
Positioned in the eyes,
Attentive for a word.

The pupils here obey
The friend's didactic voice,
Are wakeful at a smile,
Can answer questions, lie,
Express polite surprise.

If one should raise a hand,
Ask question out of turn,
Then discipline would die,
Order be broken and
The other's eye be stern.

'He thought of being in a single room'

He thought of being in a single room,
Working in shirt sleeves at a public school
Feeling unhappy and desiring change,
How he was on the nerves of all his friends
Fretting in solitude all that summer.

He knew that he had passed another summer,
Looked through the window of his single room
But least of all had he accomplished change
Although affectionate to different friends,
With memories fading of his public school.

He wondered vaguely, Was the world a school?
Running by rules and quite opposed to change,
Censoring love though not averse to friends,
From which were only holidays in summer,
Packing a trunk and stepping from a room?

Must he from fears and illness keep his room,
Afraid of words like 'intimacy' and 'friends',
Life seen from windows, there be never change?
His university was only school
Hardly made bearable by friends and summer.

The time for opening windows was in summer,
In love perhaps and not at ease with friends,
Feeling their presence discipline like school.
But he alone could never leave that room
Although disturbing winds whispered of change.

Some words haunted his brain, like 'love' and 'change',
Took on new significance in the summer.
Some words turned into phrases, 'O my room,'
'Open the windows', and this was his school
Teaching him grammar and the worth of friends.

The English Wife

He had a steady hand
   And a clear eye,
He was gay, he was bland,
   And as straight as a die.

I was never frigid,
   I was never coy,
But O he has left me
   For a pretty boy,

For a gay mechanic
   Unbuttoning overalls,
More dangerous than movies
   Or the music halls.

Once he longed for me
   And my lovely bed
And in these hands have rested
   His tired head.

And the soft exertions
   Of the velvet night
Were the bold assertions
   Of my ancient right,

The language of the body,
   The sincere saying,
No winner in the game
   That we were playing.

I was significant form
   And the fabled city,
Who now am torn
   With anger and self-pity.

I was the Ideal
   And abstract beauty,
More powerful than power
   Or sense of duty.

By accident I saw them
   In the little car,
Urged with love's secrecy
   Behind the garage door.

The wind, how it did blow!
   And the rain drumming
Delayed the bitter snow,
   The crisp snow coming.

I sheltered in the doorway
   But my heart was in the storm,
While in the azure coupé
   They were warm, so warm!

With their kissing and their fingers,
   In love's aerodrome,
At the controls I left them
   And walked home.

For hours I sat in silence
   With my numbness and my pain,
But his car was stumbling westwards
   Through the bounding rain.

He drove my happiness away
   Into red Devon,
He took the brightest angels
   Out of my heaven,

Down the motorist's roads
   To the teashops and the cream
He left me sad and single
   With a sexual dream,

An unreal incubus
  And a real sorrow
Not for to-day only
  But for to-morrow.

And in the dim city
  And the aching vein
The true reality is pity
  And the pain, the pain.

Cambridge

Imagine all the dons in the attitudes of buggers
With their complicated neurotic simplicity of learning,
Something comfortable, something not quite real,
The life of the tea-table, the book-scattered study,
The manuscript under the magnifying glass
In that white, cultured hand, deserving of pity.

Dons live on with occasional satisfaction,
Hand on the shoulder of the promising pupil,
Attracted but envious of the coming young men,
Middle age has caught them and the night comes after,
No soothing books and no charming companions
To quieten those nerves that cry for satisfaction.

What was their desire? Was it known and never realized,
Behind the lines and bathed in yellow lamplight?
In the world where their young men fight and are wounded
They suffer neglect like a curtain or a picture.
Pitying themselves they are never wounded,
Suffering quietly with a book in hand or smoking.

Miss Twye

Miss Twye was soaping her breasts in her bath
When she heard behind her a meaning laugh
And to her amazement she discovered
A wicked man in the bathroom cupboard.

John Betjeman's Brighton

For Charles Rycroft

Lovely in the winter sunshine lies the Haslemere Hotel,
Near the Homeleigh and the Sussex, home of ex-King Manoel.
Lager in the West Pier Tavern, cocktails in the Metropole,
Who can spot Lord Alfred Douglas – not the gross and
    coarse of soul!

Stained our hands, our lips polluted, with a sinful cigarette,
We who saw 'The Dance of Love' – we are not likely to forget
Those moustaches and those knickers, seen through that
    machine of shame.
Palace Pier, beloved of wavelets, hushed the breath that bears
    thy name!

We remember shouting breakfasts, old men who forgot
    their teeth,
Exchanging photographs of nurses, symptoms, means to
    gain relief.
We remember that Pavilion, Moorish, with chinoiserie,
And the Ice Rink and the High Street, Fuller's layer-cake for
    tea!

Still we see those sugar-daddies flashing by in terraplanes,
On the Hove Lawns lonely colonels fight again their last
    campaigns;

Wickedly we drank our coffee in Sherry's where the bad
    girls go,
From the balcony we watched them bathed in purple
    light below.

O Finlandia, heavenly music, played by massed bands on
    the pier,
O those automatic palmists, how I wish that I were there!
O pin tables, Russian billiards, where the ball melodious clicks,
And the languid coloured postcards, bathing-girls of 1906!

O voluptuous! O ecstatic! O that convalescent air!
In the sun those terraced houses, wonderful wonderful
    Regency Square!
There among the winds of winter we were gay in spite of gales,
Still a memory we cherish though the recollection pales.

Home

How awful to live in a horrible house
    Where there's nothing to eat but cold chicken and grouse
And there's nothing but barking and horrible noise
And the sound of a harsh, unpleasant Voice;
    Where a really fine couple of beautiful cats
    Are kept in the basement as though they were rats –
And a permanent wireless to keep us in error
By means of continued false humour and terror,
    With everything run to a penny and mean
    And everyone asking you 'Where have you been?'
Or 'Where are you going?' and 'What did you do?'
To make everyone nervous, bad-tempered and blue –
    And there's nothing but illness and feeling rotten
    And worrying over what's better forgotten,
Sadism, anaemia, anxiety neurosis
To make our dear home such a sweet bed of roses.

How awful to live where a horrible Dog
   Is pampered and petted as though he were God
And all love is destroyed but not malice and fear
Though a code of good manners still flourishes there
   And our laughter adorns such hysterical scenes
   As a meal off cold mutton, potatoes and greens.
How awful to see the same faces each day
So full of self-pity, disgust and dismay,
   To hear the same voices that say the same things
   And the dog having fits every time the bell rings –
O could one imagine an atmosphere fitter
To make one depressed, antisocial and bitter?

   Written in 1938, unemployed and living at home, full of adolescent
rebelliousness and bad temper.

Sonnet, 1940

The point where beauty and intelligence meet,
Where intersecting lines cross and divide –
Happy were I to lie between those feet
Or by that rare and warm and lovely side –
You are the centre of my moving world,
The cold ideal to which I daily move
Although iron flags of battle are unfurled –
You are not yet, though might still be, my love.
And I, before the happy tough battalions
Engulf me or the frozen seas of Norway,
Have still my dreams of cities and of dalliance,
But most of you as standing in a doorway,
Who might, though I so dissipate my life,
Be mistress or, fear of the young, a wife.

When a Beau Goes In

When a Beau goes in,
Into the drink,
It makes you think,
Because, you see, they always sink
But nobody says 'Poor lad'
Or goes about looking sad
Because, you see, it's war,
It's the unalterable law.

Although it's perfectly certain
The pilot's gone for a Burton
And the observer too
It's nothing to do with you
And if they both should go
To a land where falls no rain nor hail nor driven snow –
Here, there or anywhere,
Do you suppose *they* care?

You shouldn't cry
Or say a prayer or sigh.
In the cold sea, in the dark,
It isn't a lark
But it isn't Original Sin –
It's just a Beau going in.

Hymn to Proust

For you Time Past could not forget
   Nor alter what had been –
And Time has still its lost Odette
   And Love its Albertine.

We worship under different names
   The figures of the past,
Like characters from Henry James –
   But not designed to last.

For we know many a Charlus still
   And many a Verdurin,
Gilberte as Swann and de Forcheville,
   And M. Legrandin.

Each, an ambiguous Saint-Loup,
   Carries Françoise within,
And sex comes to its Waterloo
   In Jealousy, not Sin.

For all know Vinteuil's little phrase,
   The brilliant Balbec day,
The Méséglise and Guermantes' ways,
   The greyness of Combray.

Each one has tasted as a child
   Madeleines dipped in tea
And loves that drove the reason wild
   But set the fancy free.

Spring Song

Efficiency in offices is found
And love in basements and in two-room flats
And death traditionally under ground.

There are no new equations to propound –
Although we get as drunk and blind as bats
Efficiency in offices is found.

The Life Force, always, pushes us around
Until they lay us out like table mats
With death traditionally under ground.

Perhaps a parson black and trimly gowned
Will speak of us while friends remove their hats –
Efficiency in offices is found.

So get the girls and get the whisky downed
While we're alive we're luckier than cats
And death traditionally under ground.

Let love and beauty dance and music sound
The land be gay with lambs, the sea with sprats –
Efficiency in offices is found
And death, traditionally, under ground.

After Heine

With an Irish accent

The old malicious stories,
The hymns of love and hate:
Oh, let us see them buried
In a coffin huge and great.

For much will I lay in it
(But what, I will not say).
The coffin must be larger
Than the whole of Dublin Bay.

A monstrous bier bring also
Of boards both strong and thick;
It must be long, much longer
Than the road to Limerick.

And bring me twelve great giants –
They must be stronger far
Than Greek and groaning Atlas
Or wrestling angels are.

They must drag out the coffin,
And plunge it in the waves;
For coffins so gigantic
Must have gigantic graves.

Then say why is the coffin
So heavy and so vast?
It bears my loves and sorrows
Together in it cast.

Huckstep

Huckstep was the groundsman at my prep school.
He put the heavy roller over the pitch,
Dragged by a horse in large flat leather shoes,
In those long-vanished summers.
A handsome smiling man and sunburned; quiet;
The brownest man I'd ever seen,
Dark oily hair and powerful arms in shirt sleeves.
He played, somebody told me, for the Kent Second Eleven,
Certainly he bowled at us in the nets,
Left arm medium, round the wicket,
With a beautiful action, a back-tossed lock of hair.

Now that I've been 'literary' for so many years
I recognize him. He might have been
Lady Chatterley's lover, Ted in *The Go-Between*,
The natural man. A Kentish yeoman
Who even then charmed me with his grace –
So that for ever I shall see him bowling,
Picture the wheeling arm, the fluent action.
His name is one of those like 'Adlestrop'
That, once absorbed, can never be forgotten.
Huckstep. We all admired him.
And who, if he was as I think he was, would not?
There is a place in life for simple people.

Tennysonian Reflections at Barnes Bridge

The river flows before my door,
Sad with sea-gulls, mute with mud
Past Hammersmith and Castelnau,
And strung with barges at the flood.
Pink rowing girls by eight and four
Gently stroke the tide of blood.

A railway runs from side to side
And trains clank over on the hour.
The rowers strain and stretch and slide,
Hair like chrysanthemums, the flower
Of girlhood not yet opened wide,
Each happy in her virgin power.

The dying sun, the dying day
With sunlight charms suburban reaches,
The hackneyed river flows away,
And Time runs too, experience teaches,
Nor for the boring bard will stay
Or rowing girls as fresh as peaches.

Chelsea in Winter

It's a long pull down the King's Road and down to the
    Pier Hotel
To the Thames where the turbulent seagulls float backwards on
    the swell
As muffled in my duffle coat
Unruffled in my duffle coat
I walk the streets of Hell.

Intellectual introspective streets of the higher income brackets
Trodden by Mr Eliot's feet and the leaders of the rackets★

★ Refers particularly to portrait painters.

Where artists in their duffle coats
Feel smartest in their duffle coats
Like cigarettes in packets.

The Carlyle statue, pondering, sits wrapped in gloomy thought,
And warns that Human Wisdom still may be too dearly
    bought –
When duffle coat meets duffle coat
Each passes like a river boat
Towards its final port!

Serious Matters

A thin girl with an Earl's Court cleft
Has promised me remission of my sins.
I can't afford to die. My family need me.
What would they do if I suddenly stopped earning?

That bowler-hatted major, his face is twitching,
He's been in captivity too long.
He needs a new war and a tank in the desert.
The fat legs of the typists are getting ready
For the boys and the babies. At the back of my mind
An ant stands up and defies a steam-roller.

Striptease

They sit round us, hot from the Motor Show, these imagists.
They'll carry home a pack of coloured snaps
To be fingered over when the wife is lying asleep.
The young pink nipples, not yet stained dark
By maternity. The small patch of fur
That brings the eye down, makes long legs seem short,
Disturbing the centre of gravity.

The frantic metal music
Slices our head-tops like a breakfast egg.
Young girls. Old routine. A business
Like any other. Everything shakes like a jelly.
Oral or phallic, here the law keeps us visual.
The eyes devour – but are soon satisfied.
After a time you can get very tired of chicken
(Though they'll never believe that, back on the farm).

Wanting Out

They're putting Man-Fix on my hair. And through the window
Comes a naked woman with a big whatnot. Oops! I'm away
To a country where the fantasies can be controlled.
Modestly I want to live, modestly. Where the Herr Baron
Takes an Eiswein from the cellar, cradles it gently
In the tiny frozen hands of an echt Deutsch Mimi.
Where the quiet roebuck surround the hunting lodge,
Where the peasants, if they wanted, could shave with their hats.

Take me down to a Lustschloss in the year 1900,
Give me tea on the lawn of a vicarage garden,
Put me in a punt with all my little girl friends,
Let the dreams grow into the leafy sex-books.
I want a magnifying glass and a knowledge of Coptic

And a box in the British Museum for the last performance of
  Hamlet.

Short Time

She juliets him from a window in Soho,
A 'business girl' of twenty.
He is a florid businessman of fifty.
(Their business is soon done.)
He, of a bright young man the sensual ghost,
Still (in his mind) the gay seducer,
Takes no account of thinned and greying hair,
The red veins webbing a once-noble nose,
The bushy eyebrows, wrinkles by the ears,
Bad breath, the thickening corpulence,
The faded, bloodshot eye.

This is his dream: that he is still attractive.

She, of a fashionable bosom proud,
A hairstyle changing as the fashions change,
Has still the ageless charm of being young,
Fancies herself and knows that men are mugs.

Her dream: that she has foxed the bloody world.

When two illusions meet, let there not be a third
Of the gentle hypocrite reader prone to think
That he is wiser than these self-deceivers.

Such dreams are common. Readers have them too.

The Middle Years

Between the pale young failure
And the bloated purple success
Lie the works on the life of the dahlia
Or the shrewd financial guess.

Between the love and the yearnings
And the fat indifference of age
Lie the greatly increased earnings
And the slick best-selling page.

Between the romantic lover
And the sordid dirty old man
Lies the fruitful wasted lifetime
Of the years that also ran.

A Christmas Message

In the few warm weeks
    before Christmas and the cold
the Toy Department is organized like a factory floor.
They're using epitaxial planar techniques
    in the labs. The toys are sold
and there's rationalized packaging and at the hot core

of the moving mass
    sweats a frost-powdered Father Christmas
in a red dressing-gown and an off-white beard.
What he wants most is a draught Bass.
    On a dry Hellenic isthmus
Zeus was a god who was equally hated and feared;

England is a Peloponnese
    and Father Christmas a poor old sod

like any other, autochthonous. Who believes
in the beard and the benevolence? Even in Greece
   or Rome there is only a bogus God
for children under five. Those he loves, he deceives.

The Law Allows Cruel Experiments on Friendly Animals

I don't feel very well. I'm the head of a rebellious
Family, where everybody's shouting. Shall we ever find
The particular island where we can all be happy?
Put up the huts, shoot the goats, plant the corn.
But I'm not Mr Fix-It, the Handyman Husband,
I'm not forceful or even a Leader.
Youth is the happiest drunkenness. Sober, we see
The problems that, young, we never guessed at.
No longer drinking black champagne with blondes,
Spinning with them the desert island discs,
And bathing naked in the sparkling deep blue water.

If I hit a child in anger I feel ashamed.
Weak kings are subject to flashes of temper,
Ruled by their emotions. So are strong ones.
We're in a test tube, say the theologians.

Someone is watching. His tremendous eye
Glares at us, held up to the light.
We are a few decimals in a book.

Nobody can get out, all our behaviour
Goes down against a date and time of day.

He'll publish his results – and maybe soon.

Crossing the Bar

My ambition is to live to be eighty,
To die quiet, surrounded by branded goods,
In perfect harmony like Oxo and Katie,
In a gamekeeper's cottage in the woods.

I want to drift towards my last Bournvita,
My children happy and a room of books
With their lined agony to make comfort sweeter,
Remembering the girls and their good looks.

I want all my employment to have been gainful,
My life to be free of angst and nuclear war,
And my last illness not to be terribly painful,
As I float in towards that distant shore.

War-time

A smooth bald head, a large white body.
No trace of pubic hair.
Raw, fretted and frayed by that rocky coast,
The flesh where the nipples were.

A woman drowned in war-time
On the Ligurian shore.
An Italian shouted 'E una femmina!'
There seemed to be nothing more.

A suicide? A Resistance girl
From La Spezia floated down,
A murderee from Genoa?
The coast road into the town

Led me back to Livorno
And a British Army tea.

The war got hold of the women,
As it got hold of me.

Twenty years later, in the offices,
The typists tread out the wine,
Pounding with sharp stiletto heels,
Working a money mine.

It's a milder war, but it is one;
It's death by other means.
And I'm in the battle with them,
The soft recruits in their teens.

The Dildo

The Dildo is a big heavy cumbersome sort of bird,
Supposed extinct for many years but its voice is often heard
Booming and blasting over the marshes and moors
With the harsh note of Lesbos and the great outdoors.
The Dildo wears tweed skirts and Twenties elastic-thighed
    knickers
And smokes black cheroots and still calls films 'the flickers'.
It wears pork-pie hats and is really one of the boys,
It has initiated many pretty girls into forbidden joys.

It has an eye-glass in one eye, and its bad-taste jokes are myriad,
Such as the one about Emily Bronte's Last Period,
And a good many others that are best left unsaid,
Buried in the old laughter, as the dead bury the dead.

The Dildo is quite frankly worshipped by some members of the
    community,
Who consider that even its name cannot be taken in vain with
    impunity
As it hops heavily about on its one wooden leg –
But most real Nature-lovers think it should be taken down a
    peg.

The Masturbon

The Masturbon is a sort of dirty great elephant and it lives
   in a cave.
It's terribly keen on Do-It-Yourself, but it never bothers
   to shave.
It spends all its time reading ads and clipping the coupons out
And addressing them to itself. It knows what life's all about.
It has five spin-dryers and a twin-tub and a dream house and a
   Teasmade
And a Special Offer beach ball, and a bucket and spade
But it keeps them all at the top of a very high mountain
A long way away, too far for checking or counting.
It reads the *Daily Express*, and nothing in its life is shared.
When it dreams, it dreams in French and often shouts '*Merde!*'
At the sexiest parts of the dreams. It is very close to God,
Though its personal habits to you or me would seem
   unmentionable – or at least very odd.

The Masturbon, I must tell you, is a perfect hermaphrodite.
It sleeps during the day and comes into its own at night.
It loves dirty photographs and paws them all over
And it reads whole Police Stations-full of dirty books. It's really
   in clover
At a big swinging striptease. The music and the tits
Send it into ecstasies and mild epileptic fits.
In fact, like George the Fourth who was known as Georgy-
   Porgy,
The Masturbon's life is one long delicious orgy.

Office Friendships

Eve is madly in love with Hugh
And Hugh is keen on Jim.
Charles is in love with very few
And few are in love with him.

Myra sits typing notes of love
With romantic pianist's fingers.
Dick turns his eyes to the heavens above
Where Fran's divine perfume lingers.

Nicky is rolling eyes and tits
And flaunting her wiggly walk.
Everybody is thrilled to bits
By Clive's suggestive talk.

Sex suppressed will go berserk.
But it keeps us all alive.
It's a wonderful change from wives and work
And it ends at half past five.

Pi-Dog and Wish-Cat

When Pi-Dog and Wish-Cat sat down for a meal,
His and Hers on their bowls, there was a great deal
For them both to pronounce on, deny and discuss.
Their words were all taped and have come down to us.

Pi-Dog said he believed in a Man In The Sky
Who would end the whole world in a flaming great fry
Most delicious for dogs (who of course would be spared),
And the bones of their enemies equally shared.

Wish-Cat said, purring, how Love was the thing

And was easily captured by using a ring;
How Love would in rapture squeak louder than mice
And live happy as dreams. And wasn't it nice?

When the meal was all over they both wanted more –
And Pi-Dog dragged Wish-Cat down onto the floor.
Pi-Dog bit hard and deep, and she clawed at his eyes.
Now they both of them sleep where it says HERE LIES.

June 1966

Lying flat in the bracken of Richmond Park
while the legs and voices of my children pass
seeking, seeking; I remember how on the
13th of June of that simmering 1940
I was conscripted into the East Surreys,
and, more than a quarter of a century
ago, when France had fallen,
we practised concealment in this very bracken.
The burnt stalks pricked through my denims.
Hitler is now one of the antiques of History,
I lurk like a monster in my hiding place.
He didn't get me. If there were a God
it would be only polite to thank him.

The Statements

Arts are actually anthropomorphic.
Business is often bilaterally baleful.
Causality is a considerable cow.
Desires are delightful as well as desperate.
Energy in everything is everlasting.
Freedom is frequently fairly fallacious.
Growing girls go gay with gallantry.
History has some horrible hermits.
Illness is injurious only to idiots.
Jokes are jealous and jazz is jolly.
Kitchens are kinetic like kisses and kiwis.
Love is laudable and lately laundered.
Matrimony is mainly merry and miserable.
Names are numinous and never negligible.
Officers often open their orifices.
Palaeontology is particularly painful.
Quails are queer but quiet and queenly.
Restless rovers are rarely repentant.
Soles slide sideways in silent seas.
Terrible tornadoes torture the terrain.
Under umbrellas the uncles take umbrage.
Various virgins veer into vinegar.
Weary wallflowers wait wetly for wisdom.
Xylophones excel in extemporization.
Yelling in youth is yesterday's yawning.
Zen is as zealous as zebras and zinc.

Lifelines

In the rat race he won by a whisker.

Bitching and bitching in the double bed.

She came unexpectedly, while he was standing waiting.

A voice from a jar of vaseline: 'This too is love.'

A girl like a cat sits in the window of The Sizzling Sausage.

In the great cities the ants are actuarians.

The lips of the Muse have the taste of beauty.

In a field of alien corn a girl was reaped.

The Great Lines

For bad men do what good men only dream.

The beauties warble down the tracks of time.

What could console is working like a watch.

After the banquet: 'Shall we join the dead?'

From the wild lands the precious food of cities.

A dream of adultery: two for the price of one.

Even the wolves, at last, will go away.

Hands

With her short squat (and greedy) hands she seized power.

Yesterday he set his hand and seal
to his final arrangements for frying Boy Scouts.

Meretricious Mayfair hands were bathing the

Birmingham balls.

He wants God to lean down with an enormous hand
and slap on his back a label that says SATISFACTORY

Above the wine-shop her hands enticed him.

The writing hand was wobbling over the paper.

Classical Disasters

The brazen bull was filled with his bellowing.

The wax was melting as the wings climbed higher.

At the big banquet the food was human.

The greedy cloth bit at his muscular body.

He clubbed the old man at the lonely crossroads.

They cut the tongue from her squealing struggles.

At the last strained heave the stone toppled backwards.

Lines of History

By a deserted road the Apostles were peeing.

The sun through the burning-glass tickled the warm hay.

The sea heaved with its burden of whales.

The antheap was teeming with cries of injustice.

Above the wineshop she cupped her hands and held him.

Past the window of the torture chamber flew the pigeons.

There was no silence, now or at any time.

The Headlines

No dice, as Rasputin flies in to floozies

Mean famine tempts 5 bits from Queen

Profs flee as city falls to Turks

Agitator executed on funereal hill

Limeys and krauts combine to flog the frogs

Sage corrupts youth, say City Fathers

Too much water spoils the tea

Norman Archer catches Harold's eye

Demagogue roasts books, heebs

Daughters claim Pop unfit to rule

Allies victorious, fry Troy by stratagem

Arithmetic

I'm 11. And I don't really know
my Two Times Table. Teacher says it's disgraceful
But even if I had the time, I feel too tired.
Ron's 5, Samantha's 3, Carole's 18 months,
and then there's Baby. I do what's required.

Mum's working. Dad's away. And so
I dress them, give them breakfast. Mrs Russell
moves in, and I take Ron to school.
Miss Eames calls me an old-fashioned word: Dunce.
Doreen Maloney says I'm a fool.

After tea, to the Rec. Pram-pushing's slow
but on fine days it's a good place, full
of larky boys. When 6 shows on the clock
I put the kids to bed. I'm free for once.
At about 7 – Mum's key in the lock.

The Pseudo-Demetrius*

After the summer on the lovely island
came the pretender, the autumn of the city,
the Pseudo-Demetrius garlanded with blackberries;
the true young one had strawberries and raspberries
and the real love in the matchless bed.

After the moistness of the pink lips opening
came the equivocal, the Pseudo-Demetrius,
the one who told us he would make us equal

* In the history of medieval Russia there are two Pretenders. They are called
Pseudo-Demetrius I and Pseudo-Demetrius II.

to what we were when the flowers were young ones
and we knew love in the matchless bed.

After the sun's hour, the failing succession
came with a turbulence but no tenderness,
the anger and envy of the Pseudo-Demetrius,
the one who stirred up trouble and caused the ending
of our best love in the matchless bed.

After the green and the bees in clover
came the new season when we were forgotten,
the riot and sadness of the Pseudo-Demetrius,
brown leaves falling on the musclemen fighting,
and no real love in the matchless bed.

After the summer, after the sun's hour,
came the equivocal, turbulent pretender,
the Pseudo-Demetrius garlanded with autumn,
with lies and fighting in the darkened city,
and death, not love, in the matchless bed.

Abelam

The long-yams are being grown in honour of the moon
A critic recalls Plissetskaya's celebrated jump
Soman is somewhere in the worship of the deadly
The strikers show clever running off the ball
That harpsichord remembers Michael Haydn.

The rainbow, they say, is a snake of no importance
The audience is kinky about Khachaturian
A headline says Hendon Afternoon Dogs
Some secretaries regard themselves as debs
Caroline Quoin on Candlewick has a clear round.

The hornbill carvings are definitely phallic
Graveney is stroking the ball through the covers
A broken choirboy miscalculates some trills

Menstruating women are put in special huts
Blake is accused as a formless draughtsman.

At important ceremonies there are palm-leaf flares
The Porsches like a plague overrun the country
Some minds are tickled by the feathers of investiture
The gin is jumping from the bankers' fountains
The massed choirs are singing A.M.D.G

People Will Say We're in Love

But seriously, as the marriage wears on, thanks for the memory of hauling prams and shopping up icy door-
steps, equally as for the kisses and the dem-
onstrative eyes. Wives work hard. Cathy and her moor-
land romance are fine in the mind, but the car-
ing for babies is the real and most test-
ing fact of a union. The children are the shar-
ing. It's always Housewives *v*. The Rest.

And it's always into big offices for the good provid-
ers, the traditional way to keep the bank managers happy. Families don't like outsid-
ers. This is men's washing and ironing, fan-
ning up a little flame of money in the current account. Chores of the typewriter. Essential reading about Management. Not the true sweetness, sacc-
harine at best – a businessman's Creed.

So the success of a marriage can be seen in the children and, believe me, certainly yours is the credit, after the nappies, the orange juice, the pil-
fered hours of sleep they took from you, bedtime too often a night shift, and loving not the novelist's outspoken randy young sprawlers, pushing and shov-
ing, but tiredness, the offered and the taken hand.

Victorian

Miss with the vapours.
The claret and the oysters.
The curling papers.
Fat clergy in the cloisters.

Heavy squires hunting.
Pints of port and porter.
Grumbling and grunting.
Gothic bricks and mortar.

Fog in the dockyards.
Decorum at the Palace.
Blood in the stockyards.
Murder in the alleys.

The Select Party

Hands that wiped arses
are holding glasses,
lips that fellated
are intoxicated,
parts that were randy
have counterparts handy –

but the fact of a quorum
preserves decorum,
and the social unction
inhibits the function
of the natural passions
concealed by the fashions.

The Sentimental Education

Wear your Thomas Hardy suit and sit with candles in
    the gloom.
Summon ghosts of years departed till they fill the empty room.

First of all call up the weather – heatwave 1922,
Wartime winters with the blackout, blossom on the trees
    at Kew.

Then the people. First, a nanny. Next, your father wearing spats.
Mummy with her pearls at evening, and her three amazing cats.

Childish captions fit the pictures – you were very childish then –
But you see it still as clearly as the present world of men.

Peter Pan was pulsing drama, green lights shone on Captain
    Hook.
Carroll's Jabberwock caused nightmares, till you had to hide
    the book.

You were one. Then came two sisters. They were different
    from you.
You liked best fried bread and cocoa, loved the zebras at
    the Zoo.

Then the schools – a bourgeois saga – we all know what they
    were like.
Minnows in a pond, a bully swam among them like a pike.

Squeeze them in? You'ld need a ballroom. Still remembered,
    many names
Cluster round in shorts and sweaters. Latin, algebra and games.

Chapel services. Then freedom, and the length of King's Parade.
Dadie, Anthony – and Classics, all the dons that had it made.

Cicero made ghastly speeches, elegiacs were a bore.
You had two years in the saltmines – how could you come up
    for more?

Next was English, Richards lectures, Leavis supervising. Fine.
English literature went down as stimulating as new wine.

After Cambridge – unemployment. No one wanted much
  to know.
Good degrees are good for nothing in the business world below.

In the end you were a salesman, selling lithographic prints.
Trade was stagnant after Munich. Hitler frightened us with hints.

War came down, a blackout curtain, shutting out the kindly sun.
Jews went under, all the playboys somehow lost their sense of
  fun.

Still, we always had the weather – freezing cold or hot as hell –
Birds continued, flowers were rampant, life went on through
  shot and shell.

Back at last to shabby London, tired and rationed, sad to see,
With its tales of air raid wardens, siren suits and hot sweet tea.

People, literary people, now replaced the roaring boys
Fond of vino, signorinas, dirty jokes and lots of noise.

Tambi, Nicholas and Helen. Come on in. You see them plain.
Publishing will never, surely, be as odd as that again.

Money, said the British Council, I have money in my hand.
Get your hair cut, keep your nose clean, live in Civil
  Serviceland.

Six years later came the end game – middle grades were axed.
  Goodbye!
They were victims of the Beaver's petulant persistent cry.

Advertising. Advertising. Fatal Lady of the Lake!
No one opts for copywriting, they get in there by mistake.

You absorbed those business ethics – not the Sermon on the
  Mount –
Walked into that artful parlour, had the William Hill account.

Let the room explode with whizz kids, dollies, every kind of
   Pop!
Only crematorium silence brings that mayhem to a stop.

Money. Children. Mortgage. Rat race. Anxious words that tax
   the brain.
Nagging fears of unemployment drive the middle class insane.

It's not pretty when they throw you, screaming, in the
   empty sack,
Filled with nothing but the cries of wives and children
   screaming back.

Does the working class get ulcers? No one worries much, if so.
They know jobs are hard to come by, and the pay is often low.

They're inured to thoughts of hardship and of being out
   of work.
This is life. It's no good blubbing, throwing fits or going
   berserk.

Moneyed men in Lloyds, the City, can't imagine what it's like.
To the driver of an E-type, what's the old penurious bike?

Workmen are a bloody nuisance – just a ROAD UP sign or two –
Obstacles that spoil their record from the Bank to Luton Hoo.

Keep your voice down. Don't start shouting. Let the candles
   burn up straight.
(Privileged and trendy diners stuff themselves with After Eight.)

All you learn – and from a lifetime – is that that's the
   way it goes.
That's the crumbling of the cookie, till the turning up of toes.

2001: The Tennyson/Hardy Poem

When I am old and long turned grey
And enjoy the aura of being eighty,
I may see the dawn of that critical day
When my lightest verse will seem quite weighty.
I shall live somewhere far away,
Where the illiterate birds are nesting.
To pilgrim admirers my wife will say:
       Ewart is resting.

Instead of the heedless sensual play
And the youthful eyes of love and brightness
I shall see critics who kneel and pray
In homage – I shan't dispute their rightness –
And Supplements keen to seem okay
Will flatter me with fulsome pieces.
Scholars will put it another way:
       Ewart's a thesis.

When the aching back and the bleary eye
And the dimness and the rationed drinking,
The cold unease of the earth and sky,
Leave me no pleasures except thinking
I shall be warmed (but what will be 'I'?)
With the awe inspired by what's Jurassic,
And people will say, before I die:
       Ewart's a classic.

Soon comes the day when the stream runs dry
And the boat runs back as the tide is turning,
The voice once strong no more than a sigh
By the hearth where the fire is scarcely burning.
Stiff in my chair like a children's guy,
Simply because I have no seniors
The literati will raise the cry:
       Ewart's a genius!

Sonnet: The Only Emperor is the Emperor of Ice Cream

I want a new half million pound account
that I can bash into with hammer-headed words,
revolutionize the agency's billing, put myself
among the greatest writers of TV spots for ever,
something so classical that books on advertising
will quote it for cub copywriters: a new King Lear
but bringing consumer comfort, a Verdi
of cornflakes or detergents consoling all.

That's the way the kids get fed and clothed.
Consumer goods beget consumer goods,
the god is eaten. Self-perpetuating markets
demand our sacrifice, my bending of the mind
I offer up to cans and aerosols and packs.
Surely someday those shining gods will speak?

Sonnet: The Last Things

Of course there's always a last everything.
The last meal, the last drink, the last sex.
The last meeting with a friend. The last
stroking of the last cat, the last
sight of a son or daughter. Some would be more
charged with emotion than others – if one knew.
It's not knowing that makes it all so piquant.
A good many lasts have taken place already.

Then there are last words, variously reported,
such as: Let not poor Nelly starve. Or:
I think I could eat one of Bellamy's veal pies.
If there were time I'd incline to a summary:
Alcohol made my life shorter but more interesting.
My father said (not last perhaps): Say goodbye to Gavin.

Hurried Love

Those who make hurried love don't do so
from any lack of affection
or because they despise their partner
as a human being –
what they're doing
is just as sincere as a more formal wooing.

She may have a train to catch; perhaps the
room is theirs for one hour only
or a mother is expected back or
some interruption
known, awaited –
so the spur of the moment must be celebrated.

Making love against time is really
the occupation of all lovers
and the clock-hands moving
point a moral:
not crude, but clever
are those who grab what soon is gone for ever.

Memory Man

I'm sitting drinking Guinness
in memory of you,
on the wall is written Finis
and although the love was true –
if I were more romantic I would say sublime –
it was not a love that lasted until closing time.

The glasses are being polished
as they shout 'Last orders, please!'
and illusions are demolished

with the same fantastic ease
as the ease with which Joe closes his democratic bar –
if I think of you now, it's 'you were' and not 'you are'.

Each man that loves a woman
must be prepared for this
for a sexual love is human
and betrayal by a kiss
is a commonplace and not just in the holy Book
and it all begins when your eyes take that first long look.

You must have the boldness
to overcome the moods,
the sulking and the coldness,
your love must feed on foods
which wouldn't keep alive a common tabby cat;
no one can have *this* without an awful lot of *that*.

So it's sadly time to drink up
and let them stack the chairs –
he's a wise man who can think up
a remedy that bears
much resemblance to an answer (Venus is a jerk?);
for that holiday is over – from now on it's back to work.

The Larkin Automatic Car Wash

Back from the Palace of a famous king,
    Italian art
Making the roped-off rooms a Culture thing,
At about five o'clock we made a start,
Six teenagers squashed in. And as I drove
North from the barley sugar chimney pots
They sang the changeable teenager songs
That fade like tapestries those craftsmen wove,
But centuries more quickly. Through the knots
Of road-crossing pedestrians, through the longs

And shorts of planners' morse, the traffic lights,
   Over a hill,
Down to the garage advertising tights,
A special bargain, fast I drove on till
I drew up by the new Car Wash machine,
Pride of the forecourt, where a sign said STOP
Clear on the asphalt. In front a smaller car
Stood patiently as brushes swooshed it clean,
Whirling its streaming sides and back and top –
A travelling gantry; verticals, cross-bar.

We wound our windows up and waited there.
   In pixie green
The moving monster lifted itself clear,
The yellow brushes furled and now were seen
As plastic Christmas trees. Its wet last client
Made for the highway and it was our turn.
In gear and under. Two tenpences fed in
A slot on the driver's side. The pliant
Great brushes whirred and closed. Like yellow fern
One blurred the windscreen. Underwater thin

The Science Fiction light came creeping through
   Alien and weird
As when the vegetables invade in *Dr Who*,
Something to be amused at – almost feared.
And as the lateral brushes closed our sides,
Sweeping past steadily back, the illusion came
That *we* were moving forward; and I checked
The hard-on handbrake, thought of switchback rides
And how the effect in childhood was the same –
Momentary fear that gathered, to collect

In joy of safety. The tall half-children screamed –
   The girls at least –
Delighted to be frightened, as it seemed,
By this mechanical, otherworldly beast.
The boys made usual, window-opening, jokes.
And soon, tide-turning, the brushes travelled back,
Put our imaginations in reverse,
Though we were still. Like cigarettes and cokes

This was their slight excitement, took up slack
In time that wound by, idle. Nothing worse

And nothing better. To me it seemed so short,
    I wanted more,
I wanted hours, I wanted to be caught
In that dense undergrowth by that wet shore.
This was an exit from our boring life,
A changed environment, another place,
A hideout from the searchers. Otherness
Was that world's commonplace, a kitchen knife,
Something so usual that it had no face –
As the car dripped unnatural cleanliness.

Yes, it was jolly, *Fun for the kids* we say,
    But more than that;
For if you look at it another way
This was a notable peak where all is flat.
Into the main road by the riverside
We right-turned past the pubs that line the route
Where cheering crowds watch boat race crews go by,
Travelling with the full incoming tide.
The roof, the sides, the bonnet and the boot
Shone with new wetness. Yet the dust could lie

As thick there as before; and would, in time,
    This was reprieve.
Cars too grow old and dirty. Gin-and-lime
Perks up the guest; but all guests have to leave.
In through the main gate of the block of flats
I drove my giggling adolescent load,
And in vibrating door-slammed solitude
I parked. Under their different hats
Spiritual experiences work in a kind of code.
Did I have one? I, from this multitude?

Experience Hotel

The alcoholically inclined
who live in this hotel
are often stoned out of their mind
and only ring the bell
for bottles of that special kind
they know and love so well.

The ladies in their mules and wraps
who haunt the corridors
are knowledgeable about Dutch caps
and more discreet than whores
though not so different perhaps
behind their numbered doors.

The staff is neutral in all this
and tired from too much work
ignoring every pinch and kiss
from drunks who slyly lurk
to grope the matron and the miss
and the Manhattan clerk.

Trafalgar Day, 1972

All bathed and brindled like a brushed cat,
with a slight hangover from a literary party
(and what could be nicer than that?)

on the day that one-armed bandit finally bought it
I celebrate your sixteenth birthday;
Who (one could say) would have thought it,

when I was a neurotic sixteen at Wellington College,
that I should ever be a girl's *father*,
straining after poetry and carnal knowledge?

But there you are and here I am, and let it be believed
it was during a broadcast performance
of Mozart's *Idomeneo* that you were conceived.

So the whirligig of time brings in his revenges
(don't quote me on that one)
and something as mystical as our lost Stonehenges

has added another link to the chain of being,
making you real and believable,
and believing is (believe me) rather like seeing,

as you get stuck into *Jude the Obscure*,
in the gear of your generation;
Hardy certainly thought that Tess was pure

and said so on the title page. Though this is a concept
and a word that doesn't apply
much nowadays, and words themselves are inept

to transmit a person's quality, you've got a womanly feeling
of the kind men often lack.
That's what makes women, mainly, so appealing,

and when the hawks gather round to bully a dove
you'd be soft-hearted; and
the emotion you inspire in me could, loosely, be called love.

Fiction: The House Party

Ambrose is an Old Etonian and he
is terribly in love with a girl called Fluffy
who has Lesbian tendencies and is very attracted
to a sophisticated debutante called Angela Fondling
who was once the mistress of old Lord Vintage.

Don and Vi come to stay at the Castle
and neither of them know how looking-glasses aren't mirrors
or what wines go best with fish or even how to
handle a butter knife or talk about horses.
Don makes a joke about being unstable.

Fluffy doesn't know where to look and Ambrose
chokes on his claret. His Lordship is thinking
about a certain incident in 1930
when 'Filthy' Fynes-Pantlebury rode a bay gelding
up the main staircase and into a bathroom.

Angela is writing a book about the middle classes,
she keeps giving Don and Vi gin and depth interviews
and trying like a mad thing to understand Bradford.
Lady Vintage is pathetically faded
but she loves a young criminal in London: Reg. Ratcock.

They sometimes meet in the afternoon, on Fridays,
and smoke a lot of pot in the tenement basement.
Ambrose is thinking of taking Holy Orders,
he usually thinks of Fluffy as a very young choirboy.
Vi wants to go to the loo but she's shy about asking.

Lord Vintage has vanished into several daydreams;
he remembers well how Frank Fondling once shot a beater.
Don is getting very tired of gin. Vi wets her knickers.
Fluffy says to Ambrose: 'But what *is* a chasuble?'
And Angela keeps her tape-recorder running . . .

Fiction: A Message

'My dear fellow!' said the great poet, putting his arm affably
   round Ponsonby's neck,
'I respect your feelings for Gertrude. I realize they have
   something to do with sec
or secs or whatever they call it. Of course in my little backwater
   I haven't moved with the times –
just listen to the bells of St Josef – how I love those chimes!'

Down below, the Austrian lake reflected his agonized
   incomprehension sleepily in the sun.
'I'm at the end of my tether!' cried Ponsonby. 'But you – your
   race is nearly run –
I look to you for a message. I know that behind her spectacles
   she has the most beautiful eyes,
I've heard her playing Chopin at midnight with rapt, adoring
   cries!'

'These things are sent to try us' said Anzeiger. 'You'll find
   something in Apollonius of Rhodes,
or one of the Desert Fathers, that proves fairly conclusively that
   women are toads.'
'I've told myself so, yet I often have the most incomprehensible
   puzzling dreams.
I dream of the Kaiserhof, of milk churns, of chocolate creams.

Sometimes I run into a dark wood of feathery soft perfumed
   aromatic trees
or I'm sinking in unimaginable sweetness like honey, right up to
   my knees,
or I see Gertrude waving from a cottage with a very attractive
   rose-circled door.
I'm wearing my Norfolk jacket and, I'm ashamed to say,
   nothing more!'

'That sounds like the Flesh', pondered Anzeiger, fingering gently
   Ponsonby's fair curls.
'We know well that St Anthony was tempted in dreams by
   demons and dancing girls.

Though these apparitions, old fellow, seem so irrational, so
 disturbing, so unaccountably odd,
I think we can safely assume, in your case, they don't come
 from God.

Though, of course, He has been known to work in some really
 very mysterious ways.'
'But what shall I do?' cried Ponsonby. 'Offer it up. Just pray and
 give praise.
We'll take the pony and trap and go down on Sunday, dear boy,
 to Linz.
The Lord will lend a kindly ear to your account of your sins.'

They turned and walked towards the house, arm in arm. The
 sun had nearly set.
As they approached the pretty garden, by the last dark sentinel
 pine trees they met
Gertrude in a light summer dress, confidently smiling, friendly
 and demure.
Ponsonby smiled back. He was above her. Of that he was
 now sure.

Consoler Toujours

All bright love that strikes like lightning on our so-so lives
                is a bonus,
like the honey bees are making in their secret hives
                and the onus
to enjoy it is on us as decrepitude arrives,
                each Tithonus

remembering the years-ago girls clearly in his heart,
                not forgetting
all those faces and those kisses, every sexual part,
                heavy petting,

and each happy ending from a slow or frantic start,
        and its setting

– all those rooms that now hold others or are bulldozed down,
        flats and houses
standing tall as ghosts and ghostly in a ghostly town.
        The mind drowses
quietly on the beds and sofas, red, white, pink or brown.
        This arouses

old emotions, recollected in tranquillity.
        Thought's assizes
try the case of W or beauties B and C,
        no disguises
hide the naked A; as she is sleeping there so peacefully
        the sun rises . . .

Women count and hoard their lovers for the days ahead,
        single-bedding,
long last hours in hospitals, know towards what bed
        they are heading
and what bells will ring for them at that lonely dead
        last wedding;

theirs and ours, the lovely bodies end up in a mess
        or disgusting.
Yet these are the hands that fumbled to undo a dress,
        young and trusting
we gave sexual adoration, love and tenderness,
        June was busting

out all over like a song (and that's a fairly old
        jazz song title)
so let's remember that we had it – something gleamed like gold,
        very vital,
something beautiful and better than time's creeping cold
        sad requital.

To the Slow Drum

Beat for Auden, Wystan Hugh!
Solemn musics sound, where you
keep funereal pace with Time,
showing sorrow in a mime.
Measured steps go best with grief,
fitting for our old belief:
hurry does not chime with Death,
mourners mayn't be out of breath –
dead ones lie in that sad state,
doomed by tolling bells as 'late'.

Muted trombones, fateful brass
help the slow procession pass,
black on black and grey on grey
in the twilight of the day.
Music moved him; it is fit
we remember him by it.
Talent such as his is rare
and our singing branch is bare,
where shall we find such an one
now the feeling voice has done?

In the brilliance of his Art
noble grace-notes held their part
bringing harmonies as clear
to the convoluted ear
as the masters in their time,
making flute and oboe rhyme,
furnished for the sister Muse.
Homage that we can't refuse
we must pay to that true sound,
though the singer's underground.

Beat, drum, in the colder night!
If hysteric nuclear fright
seize us, choking, by the throat,
rabbits hypnotized by stoat,
let this be a potent spell

countering the ne'er-do-well
childishness of martial Man;
let these calm him – as they can –
systems closed and so complete
that aggression seems effete.

In that Never–Never–Land
all we know and understand
is that fantasy is fact,
locked as in a sexual act
two are seen to be as one,
play is play and fun is fun.
He could do it, let us swim
in that pool designed by him,
happily ourselves immerse
in the medium of his verse.

All our sorrow, all our fuss,
is entirely now for us,
not for him; for he achieved
more than many once believed
could be in an anxious age –
nervous eyes desert the page.
Beat, then, as the clock-hands cross,
dramatise our sense of loss
lights are down, here comes your cue –
beat for Auden, Wystan Hugh!

The Hut

That is the hut where she used to work; and there
    under the paint-peeled corrugated iron
with square small windows set in wooden frames
by thumb and spatula she played the old Art games;
    under the moon now, far from bright Orion,
in misty autumn, tenantless and bare
it stands so useless in the bleakly chilling air,
    nettle-surrounded, a falling garden shed,
and cobwebbed to the mean and spidered roof,
sad as great Abbeys – for Time is so aloof,
    indifferent to that life that once she led
when she sat smoking in that single chair.

The canvases have gone. Some empty frames odd-piled,
    African figures on the windowsill,
witness the young Slade student of shared youth,
paint-splashes hold a bitter kind of truth,
    the easel stands at ease in empty drill.
And with these things I must be reconciled.

The friends and sisters go; and all who had in that past smile
    (and some had beauty, some were bright with wit)
must forfeit health and come to this one room
as dark with memory as a Victorian tomb,
    and we must wrestle with understanding it
until from life and hope we are exiled.

Charles Augustus Milverton

see The Return of Sherlock Holmes

Lady Eva Brackwell, the most lovely debutante
    of last
season, will be married (and who dares say that she shan't?)
    to the stern
    and mast-
erly Earl of Dovercourt; a sensitive young plant
    in an urn,
    she fast,

yes, to his pure stiffness in a fortnight will be tied –
    but she
has dispatched imprudent letters, shaming to a bride,
    alas!
    to the
impecunious young squire who adorned her countryside –
    a class
    too free!

Oh, who's purloined those letters but Augustus Milverton?
    and who
's asking seven thousand pounds the lot, each sprightly one?
    What can
    Holmes do?
Though he looks like Mr Pickwick, he's a fiend – and she's
   undone!
    A man
    who knew

no compunction for his victims – a genius in his way –
    and he's
much too fond of swollen money-bags; when victims pray –
    smile, face,
    heart, freeze!
She'll be lucky if she falters out the word 'obey'!
    This case,
    Holmes sees,

needs the most oblique approach: impenetrable disguise.
    So he
becomes a gay young workman before Watson's very eyes –
    clay pipe,
    goatee –
walking out with Hampstead housemaids (Watson shows
  surprise),
    a type,
    you see,

quite above suspicion in the villain's servants' hall.
    Holmes plans
one last throw – a felony – to win or lose it all.
    This quite
    unmans
Watson. 'Think what you are doing!' Anguished, manly call!
    That night
    it pans

out well. With a first-class burgling kit, a nickel plated jemm-
y, diamond-tipped glass cutter, and adjustable keys, late,
    with true
    native phlegm
they invade the silent house. The safe! but changeful Fate,
    like you,
    my fem-

inine reader! Holmes has barely time to seize his tools
    when HE
enters. Quick! Behind the curtains! They will both look fools
    if caught –
    but how flee?
Milverton is not a man who plays the game by rules,
    his sport
    villainy.

Claret-coloured smoking jacket, big red leather chair,
    a long
black cigar. Unknowingly he sits before them there
    unperturbed.
    What's wrong?

It's far past his usual bedtime. Does he gloat on fair
    disturbed
    belles, a Mong-

olian idiot's grin upon his round blackmailer's face?
    The door!
Gentle rustle of a woman's dress. Ah, what disgrace
    could bring
    her before
this insufferable bounder, seated there so base,
    a thing
    beyond law?

It's a lady in a mantle, veiled and lithe and tall!
    'It is I.'
Handsome, clear-cut face, curved nose, dark eyebrow shading all
    the hard
    glittering eye.
straight the thin-lipped mouth set in a dangerous and small
    smile. Guard
    thyself! Fly!

Milverton, however, laughs. 'Ah, you were obstinate.'
    'And you
sent the letters to my husband, to my noble mate,
    a man
    so true
I was never worthy yet to lace his boots! In hate
    he ran
    quite through

grief's whole bitter gamut till it broke his gallant heart.
    He died . . .'
'Don't imagine you can bully me!' Her thin lips part,
    white hand
    inside,
buried in her bosom. Uncontrolled the wild fears start,
    unplanned,
    to slide

into Milverton's cold, scheming, brilliant, worldly brain,
    so clever.

'You will never wring a woman's innocent heart again,
        you will
        never
ruin lives as you ruined mine, to cause such countless pain,
        to kill,
        or ever

boast of those disasters that it was your trade to bring
        to our
gentle sex. Take that, you hound! Take that, you poisonous
    thing!'
        Oh, stare!
        Oh, cower!
See the little gleaming pistol emptied in the ting-
        ling air!
        Her hour,

joyfully she takes revenge! 'You've done me.' Still he lies.
        Intent,
she grinds a fashionable heel into the upturned eyes.
        Night air,
        passion spent,
the fair avenger leaves the room to Holmes and Watson, spies
        who share
secrets meant

for no one but that Justice who must still protect the weak.
        Oh, quick!
open safe and burn the letters, excitement at its peak!
        Escape
        in the nick
of time and run two miles, no breath or even need to speak,
        dim shape
        s night-thick!

Solemn in the morning Baker Streetwards comes Lestrade
        with news
of most unusual murder, masked marauders; seeks their aid.
        Holmes says
        'I refuse'.

Later, though, in Oxford Street they see the photo of a lad-
   y, gaze
   and muse . . .

Beauty with a bright tiara on her noble head,
   regal,
stately, Court-robed lady, eyebrows strongly marked, well-bred,
   nose curve
   of eagle.
Could time-honoured titles shoot a fellow mortal dead
   or swerve
   to the illegal?

Professor Otto Lidenbrock* to Wystan Hugh Auden

(as of 29 September 1974)

   You were a rare one indeed –
in crabbed Runic letters from Iceland
   you put your message across

   early, when Terror abroad
demanded the bardic responses.
   Arne Saknussem alas!

   with his alchemical lore
could never have flummoxed the Axis;
   Snorro Turleson too once

   wrote of the foreigner's rule,
a country so banjaxed by Norway.
   Gehlenites, fangasites still

   (walking-on parts, without speech)
and our titanite of zirconium,

---

* In Jules Verne's *Journey To The Centre Of The Earth* (1864), Professor
Lidenbrock is the leader of the expedition.

minerals both of us loved,
    neutral, embellish the stage.
That's why we now hold them, inhuman,
    in unregenerate hands;

    we change much faster than they,
and people have called rocks eternal.
    You, by one year, are diffuse.

I saw the light of my day
one hundred and ten years ago now,
    yes, quite eccentric and odd,

    much given to anger; they said
my sharp nose attracted iron filings –
    students don't have much respect.

Diesel and Daimler and Benz
by no means had caused the commotion
    later you found so ungay –

    skies were for poets and birds,
our roads weren't as straight but quite fumeless,
    beam engines still were around.

That was the so-simple scene
that one could call Middle Industrial.
    You'd have been happy, I know,

    in that mechanical peace
before we had jet-lag and nylon.
    Odd you most certainly were,

    not one to welcome the brash
insensitive probe of the bedroom;
    I was a funny one too.

Liking to think that we share
a true geological mania,
    comrade, I send you my peace!

Incident, Second World War

(In Memoriam P. M. B. Matson)

It was near the beginning of that war. 1940 or '41,
when everything was fairly new to almost everyone.
The bombing of cities we understood, and blackouts; and
   certainly, thanks
to the German Army and Air Force, we'd seen dive-bombers
   and tanks.
But when the fighters came in to strafe with hedge-hopping
   low attacks
how many bits and pieces would be picked up to fill the sacks?
Aircraft cannon were not much fun for the weary grounded
   troops
and there wasn't much entertainment when the Stukas were
   looping loops
but nobody knew for certain the percentage who wouldn't get
   up,
how many would be donating their arms or their legs to Krupp.
So somebody in an office had the very bright idea,
why not set up an Exercise: machine-gunning from the air?
The War Office would know exactly the kind of figures
   involved,
an exciting statistical problem could be regarded as solved.

In a field, they put khaki dummies, on the reverse side of a hill.
And afterwards, they reckoned, they could estimate the kill.
Opposite these was the audience, to watch the total effect,
a sort of firework display – but free – the R A F being the
   architect.
All arms were represented? I think so. A grandstand seat
was reserved for top brass and others, a healthy open-air treat;
enclosed, beyond the dummies, they stood (or sat?) and smoked
or otherwise passed the time of day, relaxed as they talked
   and joked.

An experienced Spitfire pilot was briefed to fly over low
and give those dummies all he'd got – the star turn of the show,
with all the versimilitude of a surprise attack.

Then to his fighter station he would whizz round and back.
They waited. And suddenly, waiting, they saw that angel
   of death
come at them over the hillside. Before they could draw breath
he passed with all guns firing; some fell on their faces, flat,
but the benefit was minimal that anyone had from that.
He reckoned that *they* were the dummies, in his slap-happy
   lone-wolf way,
that trigger-crazy pilot. He might have been right, some say.
But bitterness and flippancy don't compensate for men's lives
and official notifications posted to mothers and wives.

Nevertheless, there *were* results; percentages were worked out,
how 10 per cent could be written off, the wounded would
   be about
50 per cent or so. Oh yes, they got their figures all right.
Circulated to units. So at least that ill-omened flight
was a part of the Allied war effort, and on the credit side –
except for those poor buggers who just stood there and died.

Ending

The love we thought would never stop
now cools like a congealing chop.
The kisses that were hot as curry
are bird-pecks taken in a hurry.
The hands that held electric charges
now lie inert as four moored barges.
The feet that ran to meet a date
are running slow and running late.
The eyes that shone and seldom shut
are victims of a power cut.
The parts that then transmitted joy
are now reserved and cold and coy.
Romance, expected once to stay,
has left a note saying GONE AWAY.

Poets

It isn't a very big cake,
some of us won't get a slice,
and that, make no mistake,
can make us not very nice
to one and all – or another
poetical sister or brother.

We all want total praise
for every word we write,
not for a singular phrase;
we're ready to turn and bite
the thick malicious reviewers,
our hated and feared pursuers.

We feel a sad neglect
when people don't buy our books;
it isn't what we expect
and gives rise to dirty looks
at a public whose addiction
is mainly romantic fiction.

We think there's something wrong
with poets that readers *read*,
disdaining our soulful song
for some pretentious screed
or poems pure and simple
as beauty's deluding dimple.

We can't imagine how
portentous nonsense by A
is loved like a sacred cow,
while dons are carried away
by B's more rustic stanzas
and C's banal bonanzas.

We have our minority view
and a sort of trust in Time;
meanwhile in this human zoo

we wander free, or rhyme,
our admirers not very many –,
lucky, perhaps, to have any.

Yorkshiremen in Pub Gardens

As they sit there, happily drinking,
their strokes, cancers and so forth are not in their minds.
Indeed, what earthly good would thinking
about the future (which is Death) do? Each summer finds
beer in their hands in big pint glasses.
And so their leisure passes.

Perhaps the older ones allow some inkling
into their thoughts. Being hauled, as a kid, upstairs to bed
screaming for a teddy or a tinkling
musical box, against their will. Each Joe or Fred
wants longer with the life and lasses.
And so their time passes.

Second childhood; and 'Come in, number eighty!'
shouts inexorably the man in charge of the boating pool.
When you're called you must go, matey,
so don't complain, keep it all calm and cool,
there's masses of time yet, masses, masses . . .
And so their life passes.

Yeats and Shakespeare

Somebody wrote somewhere (about Yeats)
how even in those wasp-waisted days
before the First World War
(for twenty years reckoned among the Greats)
he was so spoiled by worship and by praise
he couldn't behave naturally any more,

as hostesses crept up behind his back
with every kind of social, sexual net
and pecking order snare;
a lion with hyenas on his track
or hunters closing in, they say, and yet
he never seemed to find this hard to bear.

Shakespeare was not so honoured in his life
though (for a player) he ended rich,
great ladies didn't swoon
to hear or see him; and a bitter wife,
it is presumed, told him the what and which
of all his faults, and told him pretty soon.

Arnold was John the Baptist, coming late
to smooth the way for universal awe,
but one thing he got right:
Shakespeare was lucky not to be thought great
outside the Mermaid, or above the law.
It's best for geniuses to travel light.

Swarm Over, Death!

(Jannice Porter. Slough Crematorium. 20 December 1974)

The planes are roaring at Heathrow
like lions at a zoo,
above Stoke Poges, near and low,
whose churchyard holds a clue
to what it is we still don't know
and what we have to do.

Under the warm and leafless bough
of this pre-winter time
we zero in to dismal Slough
as witness to a crime –
departure from our here and now
of one no wit or rhyme

can possibly in joy recall
from that uncharted state.
If God's responsible for all
(unless you call him Fate)
he seems revengeful for that Fall
and neither soon nor late

his crematoria give up,
consolatory, a ghost.
Bitter for kids, a Kiddie Kup
prepared; like flaming toast,
a sudden flare, a quick kerflup!
mums vanish. At the most

hygienic, I suppose you'd say;
but for survivors sad,
who don't forget a better day
when Friendship made them glad,
Love and Affection came to stay
and a good time was had

by one and all. The words seem trite,
like brandnames, not inspired,

like golf balls simply called Kro-Flite
(imagination tired)
or Samuel watches: Ever-rite.
We are not lit or fired

by any mystic inner glow.
We envy, everywhere,
the animals who just don't know
or, if they know, don't care –
who go because they have to go
in face of Death's blank stare.

If all's ordained, as some will say,
(we start the little cars
and in our groups we drive away)
by God or by our stars,
it isn't very fair or gay
or arguable in bars.

The One-time Three-Quarter Remembers the Past

Pulling on a clammy jersey from a prep school locker
and the boots with dry earth caked round leather studs
and after a defeat to hear the bitter précis
of the mad and shell-shocked master.

This was the game that I found more fun than soccer
and a bright day meant good running, with the ball
easy to handle, neither wet nor greasy;
wind distracting, mud disaster.

We came after a war where the terrifying word Fokker
embodied something as beastly as the opposing teams
we hated and feared; now we walk slowly,
it is time that moves much faster.

So on a bright morning we know, though age is a mocker,
that the afternoon's International will be played fast;
we run now in our minds only,
old chairs, with one loose caster.

The Second Coming

I say the Sphinx was the Boston Strangler;
and He will be born again in Oklahoma
(I shall wear the feathers of the blue crane,
which are the mark of a great warrior)
and all over the campus the boys in sneakers
will do him peculiar acts of homage,
not forgetting the earlier avatar.

A sign will be seen in Anne Hathaway's cottage.
As I walked through the wilderness of this world
I knew He would be hatched from a hen's egg
with a preference for soils that are argillaceous
and a liking for hominy grits and grapefruit.
I put on pride as a kind of humbleness
to announce a new wonder among the libraries.

I shall purify myself in a kraal or igloo,
refusing the offered breasts of the women,
it's all in the small print in my contract,
microfilmed on my brain; and His Word is sacred.
On the third day I shall emerge to testify
a miraculous birth, for the Muse a boyfriend
and for us a new speech and a life-enhanced language.

A Personal Footnote

'In addition, he will give you seven women, skilled in the fine crafts,
Lesbians whom he chose for their exceptional beauty . . .'
The Iliad, Book 9.

Nobody has ever offered
to give me seven Lesbians –
though I was once a warrior
for six long years,
slept in a tent too
on a sparse camp bed.

Somehow I missed the
spoils of the cities.
I was not important.
A silly Lieutenant
can't sulk and get
away with it

like grandiose Achilles.

To Lord Byron

on the occasion of the 150th anniversary of his death, commemorated at
the Victoria and Albert Museum

You didn't much like relics. The 'lying bust'
    seemed to you too impersonal and cold
to represent warm flesh, whose love and lust
    even the Puritans share (when not too old)
before they crumble into decent dust.
    What would *you* think of this? Would you feel 'sold'?
For geniuses, alas, it's a tradition
to end up as a paying Exhibition.

So here are portraits of that gang you banged,
    the bright, unstable, intellectual ladies;
evidence that an ancestor was nearly hanged
    (to roam, unblessed, the further shores of Hades),
that in the Lords you once stood and harangued
    and kept a bear at Cambridge. A bill (paid?) is
exhibited as proof (bear food and lodging) –
though, through your life, your debts were not for dodging.

Here, from Miss Chaworth to La Guiccioli,
    with delicate miniatures and locks of hair,
are philosophical ladies, prophetic, Nietzschely,
    high-waisted with their bosoms raised and bare –
but also bakers' wives, untamed, unteacherly,
    one that was married to a gondolier.
That auburn curl (for some peculiar reason)
of Lady Caroline Lamb gave me a *frisson*.

Pathetic, too, to read Allegra's letters
    in copybook Italian, guided by nuns,
who went to join her elders and her betters
    under those feverish Mediterranean suns
at five years old. *Caro Papa*. Hounds, setters,
    horses you kept. Children were shunned like duns.
Shelley, a guest at your Venetian palace,
was right to be angry and to call you callous.

But who am I to take a stance that's moral?
    Your entourage was not for little girls.
In any case it's far too late to quarrel –
    you were worth fifty of *our* Lords and Earls,
in days when atom bombs shake ocean coral
    we are the swine to whom you cast your pearls,
you stand like some far-shining distant lighthouse.
And what would you have thought of Mrs Whitehouse?

Would you be keen on Peter Pan and Wendy
    or anything that's cosy, coy or twee?
Contrariwise, would you admire what's trendy
    (you were a fashion once yourself) or see
virtue in what's suburban or weekendy?

To you, who only knew one kind of tea,
who never knew what roaches or a jag meant,
I dedicate this small Byronic fragment.

Sonnet: Carson McCullers

To go into your South, a different life.
Sowbelly and cornbread with syrup poured over it;
or fried slices of side meat, collard greens, hoecakes.
To go back and away towards the lonely freaks
who can't communicate, who never communicate,
and live on that diet of misunderstanding –
poor whites, poor blacks, who never get the message.
And what, for that matter, would ever be the message?

We all are freakish, mutes with hand signals;
even the most talkative outgoing lady
tells more about herself than what is actual.
Like the hot Italian *Mezzogiorno*
your country was richest in superstition.
Where you were a one-eyed person, they were blind.

The Gentle Sex (1974)

On Tuesday, 23 July,
in that black sectarian Belfast
under a rainy, cramped and hopeless sky
five Loyalist women at last,
after a false alarm visit the previous day,
found Anne Ogilby in her home; under overcast
weather, in a little car, they drove her away,

leaving behind her five-year-old daughter Sharlene, who
    could only scream and cry.

            Leader of the Women's UDA,
            Lilly Douglas was in charge.
        For questioning, to hear what Anne had to say
            (for cloudy suspicions were looming large
    over the little terraced houses of Sandy Row,
    full of memories of unemployment and bread and marge)
        why food-parcel money, that by rights should go
on food for her boy friend in Long Kesh, had gone (they
    claimed) astray.

            Each month £10.
            One of the women accusing,
        who hunted her down, we could say, like hounds,
            found it far from amusing
    that her husband was the boy friend who had lived with Anne
    for a full three months before arrest, refusing
        to return home, father of Anne's baby, a man
who had had enough of her and her marital life − that's how
    it sounds.

            They drove to a Loyalist club
            and questioned her, hard and mean;
        but then a UDA man from a pub
            happened to intervene −
    this was lucky for her indeed, and it certainly fell
    out luckily that he should have come on the scene.
        At a bus station by the Europa Hotel
they left her, released; as scared cats leave birds and dive under
    a shrub.

            A dark 31-year-old,
            unmarried mother of four;
        and even a British soldier, the women told,
            was father of one, a whore
    they couldn't call her, pots don't call kettles black,
    but they also said, and protested, a very great deal more
        about betrayed gunmen; a Protestant murder attack
she had witnessed, and the 'kneecapping' of a sheep that
    tried to leave the fold.

Just after 10.15
Lilly Douglas's teenage daughter
and another girl, only sixteen,
    stood in front of her bus and caught her.
They dragged her off. In a small red Fiat, nine
women started off to a 'Romper Room' in that quarter
    where their traitors are disciplined – fine
for the beaters-up but for the others the fun isn't so good
and clean.

    But, before they arrived, the car
    was stopped by police, who took
them all back to the bus station; so far
    no crime – so whom could they book?
Anne, the police say, kept nervously biting her nails
but refused to make a complaint (though she did look
    Like someone in need of help. Law fails
always where the community knows, and won't tell,
    who the killers are.

    At 10.30, then, next day
    (home in the small hours) she
failed to attend at the Welfare; but they
    know she was there at three.
Meanwhile, in the Elm Bar, a 'heavy squad' was drinking –
'Bumper' Graham, three unemployed teenage girls. The key
    to the whole situation, the woman of action and thinking
was 41-year-old Lilly, smuggler, forger, violent, drunk,
    brothel-keeper (police say).

    Convicted, too. Gave order:
    Graham to fetch Anne from Welfare.
He went. Without force, no lawless marauder,
    found her and took her from there.
The welfare officers had not even, then, been seen.
In an Edinburgh hostel, safe in their care,
    a place had been found, for both Anne and Sharlene.
This she never knew. Of such missed trains and wrong
    destinations Time's a relentless hoarder.

    But now: the Romper Room. And,
    when Sharlene began to cry,

71

Graham put 10p into her childish hand,
     said she'd see Mammy bye and bye
and told her to go out and buy herself some sweets.
Her mother was blindfolded with a tea towel; we know why
     a dark brown bag was put over her head. In the streets
meanwhile life flowed easy in the uneasy city, like the sea
     lapping the sand.

     Etty Cowan, Chrissie Smith, Joey Brown
          wearing, all three, white masks
made from one of Joey's jumpers (put down,
     it sounds like a game; but such tasks
come easy in the boredom and poverty of their existence),
     walked in and began to 'romper' Anne. Who asks,
          in such circumstances, exactly why? No resistance
was offered as she was pushed and kicked from one to the
     other – like a circus clown.

          Graham and Joey were upset
     by now. They tried to stop it.
But Etty Cowan was in her stride, all set,
     took a brick and wouldn't drop it,
stood over Anne and banged it on her face,
     as hard as she could, a very determined moppet.
          She and Chrissie stopped for a smoke. Some minutes' grace
she had from that; but soon they began again, giving it all
     they'd got – or could get.

          Outside the door Sharlene,
     back with a chocolate biscuit, screamed
(inside, her mother screamed; obscene
     thumps, thuds, gurgles seemed
the soundtrack of a nightmare, 'Mammy, I want my Mammy!'
echoed outside, a bad dream crudely dreamed),
     through the brown bag perhaps the blood oozed, jammy –
until she twitched no longer; even for those avengers, the slate
     wiped clean.

          So when they knew that she'd died
     they went for a bottle of wine.

They just shooed Sharlene outside
        and onto the streets. The deep mine
of vengeance was plumbed, the boil lanced.
The body? Disposed on a motorway. Fine.
        They got into a disco and danced.
For a good cause, and a mother's jealousy revenged, can make
    you feel warm inside.

            Oedema of the brain,
        associated fractures of the skull,
        and on the scalp the deepened main
            sixteen separate wounds. Dull
    their lives must have been, dull and dull indeed
    for this to be their pleasure! The wayward gull
        floats over Belfast; animals have no need
for torture. Her face was completely black. And
    certainly, chewing gum in court, they'd do it again.

*'The Lion griefs loped from the shade And on our knees
their muzzles laid, And Death put down his book'*

            Don't worry,
    poetry won't be as good as that again in a hurry!
            New 'schools', now,
    may regard us as a collection of old fools now,
            or wonder
    what on earth we saw in it – but, no blunder,
            what Bach had
    (strict formal beauty), what *The Hunting of the Snark* had,
            corroding
    and surreal anxiety, a sense of foreboding,
            and, in it
    all too, the urgency of the actual historical minute –
            these made it
    more compelling than the craftsman's ear by which he played it.

            Each age, I
    submit, has its own particular Journey of the Magi;

73

                    they carry
the gifts that alone can truly, faithfully, marry
                    the ideal
to our hesitating, wavering sense of what is real.
                    So Auden
threw round the political nasties a sort of cordon,
                    immunizing
us against their infecting presence, and rising,
                    a champion,
a serious singer, a warner, a Baptist, a Campion
                    with social
significance (a prophet whose 'Woe!' shall
                    be ignored – as
it always is – no more regarded than Harry Lauder's
                    brash singing)
came at us like Carroll's Bellman with that bell he was ringing!

                    Swinburne too
once with the young men at Oxford certainly had his turn – to
                    be chanted
in evening streets. For some sort of Saviour is wanted.
                    Dogmatics
are twenty years old, with bats in their belfries and attics,
                    a top storey
that leans, not to work or moderation, but to death and glory,
                    new magic –
Auden's wonderful hybrid rose that crossed the comic with
    the tragic.

Home Truths

What the censorious wives,
the ones who throw words like knives,
have never understood
is how it's the hen that pecks –
not the hope of better sex –
makes men leave home for good.

By ravenous sirens misled
into an alien bed?
Not so. The better lay
might be in domestic sheets
and it's not for erotic treats
husbands go on their way.

A truly nasty remark
in the conjugal dark
can act as a potent spur –
he only wants to escape,
in any form or shape,
the flying of the fur.

He longs for a different diet –
a little peace and quiet;
and to be always told
how he's an also-ran
and really hardly a man
makes him feel very old.

The Other Woman waits,
and she's not hurling plates
or thinking him inept
or running a permanent quiz;
it's him, just as he is,
she will accept.

The stir of a woman's tongue
has got some good men hung
in more vindictive days.

Trouble is what it stirs —
not his alone, but hers —
there's death in a phrase.

Oh, Darling!

'Oh, darling, I've brought you a present,
    it's here by the side of the bed,
by your beautiful plump naked bottom
    and your beautiful feminine head.
Move over and let me show you,
    reclined like an odalisque there
with your breasts like two soft circles
    and triangular pubic hair.'

'Oh, darling, it looks Victorian!
    Such a box! of such lovely wood!
Is it mother of pearl at the corners?
    You have always understood
how a woman adores *surprises*!
    and the nice unexpected things
(like red roses, a film, or a theatre)
    are exciting as diamond rings!'

'Oh, darling, I wanted to please you,
    I went to a very good shop
to buy something to keep us together
    and ensure that our loves never stop.
It's a gift of the gods — you could call it
    a bond that binds more than a kiss —
among all of the other antiques there
    there was nothing as fine as this!'

'Oh, darling! But how does it open?
    It looks so polished and clean —
but is there a key to go with it,
    or do you press something? I mean,

I can't see a sign of a keyhole.
  Oh, it *slides*! How ingenious, dear!
Let me move a bit, so I can kiss you –
  but *please* don't bite my ear!'

'Oh, darling, you've taken the lid off,
  so tell me at once what you see –
for you it may not have the meaning
  that it has, never doubt it, for me!
It is more than a beautiful symbol,
  it's a practical means to an end,
it's a lover whose love is eternal
  and a permanent faithful friend!'

'Oh darling, you've loved me and kissed me,
  you've shown me a barrel of fun,
and a thousand good times with your ardour,
  so why – now – do you show me a *gun*?
I can see it's an old-fashioned pistol,
  it's lovely, but has it been fired?
With such things, I must tell you, my darling,
  I'm really a terrible coward!'

'Oh, darling, I asked. It's a virgin,
  as it lies there with its deathly gleam,
and nobody yet has exploited
  its potential, fulfilling the dream!
As it lies there, on pale lilac velvet,
  so snugly indented, so cold,
don't you see it is Love, even Youth, there –
  and a charm against us growing old!'

'Oh, darling, But why do you glare so?
  Is it *loaded*? I guess by your eyes!
They are savaging me, sad and lion-like!
  This is quite an *unpleasant* surprise!
I was glad (it's aimed at me! Oh, Heaven!)
  to assist in the sexual act
(Please, please, darling, don't pull the trigger!)
  but *not* in a Suicide Pact!'

The Thirties Love Lyric

I follow you in my mind,
I see you each day,
how you go on your way,
and I watch you so fai-
thfully then,
as you walk about among men!

If they should pinch your behind
or stroke a big boob
in the closely-packed Tube
that would just be the Rub-
icon, when
you walk so aloof among men!

I'm with you now in the spirit, close,
so near you – though we're parted –
and I don't need to be too verbose
to say I'm broken-hearted . . .

My thoughts follow you as you find
your sweet way to the office and all of those coff-
ees, they stick close as toff-
ees, dear, when
you go out to work among men!

I still watch over you, kind,
(though it seems very trite)
when you come home at night –
avoid boys who get tight,
darling, then
you might live so safe among men!

You are the fruit, I'm the rind,
and I'm there to protect
though the worst I expect
is you won't be select-

ive, quite, when
you're offered the friendship of men!

I'm never far, though I'm miles away,
I see you very clearly,
I'm counting hours till that distant day
when I'm more than Yours sincerely . . .

These are the links that can bind –
though the boss is your type,
with blue eyes and a pipe,
please ignore all his hyp-
erbole – then
you'll still be mine among men!

A Wee Sang for St Andrew's Day

Wha dreams that I am nae a Scot,
Yon is a blastit Hottentot,
A rude uneducatit clot –
    In Southron speech –
Lang may his cods unusit rot,
    Craibs bite his breech!

May nae wlonk wink him wi' her ee,
May mini-sarks his presence flee
An' houghmagandie sic as he
    Ay strang avoid;
His lume til that he comes to dee
    A' unemployed!

I canna thole sic wallidrags –
Auld Scots an' new my Musie brags,
She can blaw baith on tartan bags
    Wi' canty mou';
The Saltire's on the best 'o flags
    When I am fou!

What though I live by London's wa'?
I ken richt weil the waups that ca'
The hairts o' Scots, aye, ane an' a',
   Baith rich an' puir;
I ken too Celtic an' fitba',
   The burn an' muir.

Sae let nae daft presumptuous loon
Wha's plaid's a stiflin' word-cocoon
Preach Lallans tae me, late an' soon.
   There's mony a sang
In mony a tongue aneath the moon –
   And nane is wrang!

GLOSSARY

cods	*balls*
craibs	*crabs*
wlonk	*lovely lady*
mini-sarks	*shortie nighties*
	(cf. 'cutty sark')
houghmagandie	*fornication*
lume	*penis*
thole	*endure*
wallidrags	*weaklings*
bags	*bagpipes*
canty	*happy*
mou	*mouth*
fou	*drunk*
waups	*curlews*
fitba'	*football*
Lallans	*Lowland Scots*

The Immense Advantage

"'I was thinking you might like gooseberry tart and cream for a sweet, miss."

'Oh that I could have vented my New World enthusiasm in a shriek of delight as I heard those intoxicating words, heretofore met only in English novels!'

KATE DOUGLAS WIGGIN, *A Cathedral Courtship* (1893)

'A hundred years ago, England had over America what Emerson called "the immense advantage". American thoughts, he wrote, were English thoughts. Today it would be as true to say that America has the advantage over Europe.'

STEPHEN SPENDER (1973)

Aw, shit, man!
What's England compared to Whitman?
Or being British
(though DHL was so cuntish and tittish)?
Even Creeley
is as way-out to *them* as stoned Swahili,
great bearded Ginsberg
is a frightening outer suburb of old-time Sinsburg.
All effete cultures
wind up, as they should, in the claws of the vultures.

I intention
to nominate the whole gang as a lavender convention,
once-English Auden
a has-been golden oldie as square as Trollope's Warden.
'Be a Star-screwer!'
yelled Corso, fuck-holes mesmerized McClure –
that's good yelling!
& fuck the Past and all punctuation and spelling!
yeah, rhyme is
far better left to those effeminate limeys.

Old Blakey
was a throbbing poet-guru and no mistakey,
like me – bearded –

and he saw the cockeyed world like no other seer did.
They don't dig, son,
though there are traces of Early American in old Geoff Grigson,
a few imitators
have raised the Stars and Stripes among those masturbators –
but don't bet on it,
most of those creeps are still writing the fucking Sonnet!

As a scene it's crappy –
no wonder those faggy Britlits are so unhappy.
The parameters
only allow them to get high on iambic pentameters –
if A-M-E-R-I-C-A
went down on them with a passio hysterica
they'd be so excited
their cocksucking pin-striped pants would get ignited!
They'd be creaming
with continuous wall-to-wall high-pitched screaming!

Don't dig Dallas,
don't dig Zukovsky's improvements to Catullus,
don't dig Berryman,
get hooked on the novels of H. Seton Merriman –
believe me, buddy,
if they tried (and they do try) they couldn't be more
    fuddy-duddy.
It's overshoes and mufflers
for that bunch of arthritic motherfucking snufflers.
AMERICA, be up and doing!
let's take a goddam trip, let's get Star-screwing!

'It's Hard to Dislike Ewart'

– New Review *critic*

I always try to dislike my poets,
it's good for them, they get so uppity otherwise,
going around thinking they're little geniuses –
but sometimes I find it hard. They're so pathetic
in their efforts to be *liked*.

When we're all out walking on the cliffs
it's always pulling my coat with 'Sir! Oh, Sir!'
and 'May I walk with *you*, Sir?' –
I sort them out harshly with my stick.

If I push a few over the edge, that only
encourages the others. In the places of preferment
there is room for just so many.
The rest must simply lump it.
There's too much sucking up and trying to be clever.
They must all learn they'll never get round *me*.
Merit has nothing to do with it. There's no way
to pull the wool over my eyes, *no* way,
no way . . .

The Semantic Limerick According to the Shorter Oxford English Dictionary (1933)

There existed an adult male person who had lived a relatively short
time, belonging or pertaining to St John's,* who desired to commit
sodomy with the large web-footed swimming birds of the genus
Cygnus or subfamily *Cygninae* of the family *Anatidae*, characterized
by a long and gracefully curved neck and a majestic motion when
swimming.

* A College of Cambridge University.

So he moved into the presence of the person employed to carry burdens, who declared: 'Hold or possess as something at your disposal my female child! The large web-footed swimming-birds of the genus *Cygnus* or subfamily *Cygninae* of the family *Anatidae*, characterized by a long and gracefully curved neck and a majestic motion when swimming, are set apart, specially retained for the Head, Fellows and Tutors of the College!'

The Semantic Limerick According to Dr Johnson's Dictionary (Edition of 1765)

There exifted a person, not a woman or a boy, being in the firft part of life, not old, of St John's,* who wifhed to —— the large water-fowl, that have a long and very ftraight neck, and are very white, excepting when they are young (their legs and feet being black, as are their bills, which are like that of a goofe, but fomething rounder, and a little hooked at the lower ends, the two fides below their eyes being black and fhining like ebony).

In confequence of this he moved ftep by ftep to the one that had charge of the gate, who pronounced: 'Poffefs and enjoy my female offspring! The large water-fowl, that have a long and very ftraight neck, and are very white, excepting when they are young (their legs and feet being black, as are their bills, which are like that of a goofe, but fomething rounder, and a little hooked at the lower ends, the two fides below their eyes being black and fhining like ebony), are kept in ftore, laid up for a future time, for the fake of the gentlemen with Spanish titles.'

* A College of Cambridge University.

Sonnet: Brief Encounter

Did we really make that journey to Northampton?
In pursuit of that coloured abortionist who did the first one?
He was very nice, you said, and had a cocktail cabinet,
and seemed clean. Two children, you said,
were quite enough for one lifetime – though I don't think any
of this did you much good, physically. I waited an hour
in the Station buffet. Then you came back, suffering
a state of shock, shivering. I bought you a whisky.

I did some shoe advertising once for a firm in Northampton.
Northampton is where they make shoes. They're fertility
   symbols
(think of the old woman who lived in a shoe).
They're wombs and vaginas. 'Something you put your foot in'
I remember hearing a psychiatrist, once, say.
You felt very cold, in the train back to London.

Sonnet: At the Villa Madeira

So I sit here, in a comfortable chair, waiting
for the three bangs on the head with a wooden mallet
that will auction me, as it were, to Eternity.
I wear my long nightcap (nearly a bottle of whisky)
each night – and, later, a conventional Counsel
will call me a *mari complaisant*, something not very nice.
But really I neither know nor care what they get up to.
I was successful, and now I'm very depressed.

We get on well enough, with friendliness.
The times are bad (the times are always bad),
I sleep downstairs. We drink a bit – that's true.
I'm 67, she's 38, and he's 18.
These are all dangerous ages. Hypocrites in wigs
will make us ogres, who prove the power of love.

Sonnet: Afterwards

When I am gone, the whole satirical setup
will carry on as before – into the foreseeable future
the world will fill itself like a basin of water
with all the archetypes. The lonely, the mother-fixated,
the psychopaths, the deviants. The big superstitious religions
will enrol from birth their thousands and tens of thousands.
The smug, the respected, the cheer-leaders, the purse-proud.
People will still believe it is right to kill people.

I shall have done little enough to improve the cosmos –
my political influence nil, my personal kindness
only a drop in an ocean where already the children
are born who will commit the next century's murders,
my love so transient it's pathetic. They'll say (if I'm lucky):
He wrote some silly poems, and some of them were funny.

Exits

If you imagine life as a large room,
most of the Exits are marked Painful –
and this is what causes fear,
to get from here to there
the despot, the dandy and the duffer
all have to suffer.

But with the sudden atomic boom –
this is what makes some men disdainful
of death – or the slick quick knife
or shot, you're out of life
like that! bingo! couldn't be faster!
And that's no disaster.

It's when the slow darknesses loom,
the clouds look doom-laden and rainful,

86

that lightning hysterias fly
across the agonized sky.
Long illness brings dreams of funerals, hearses –
but sudden death: mercies.

Don't mourn them, like some stolid marble tomb,
those who go out like a light – gainful
it isn't, and they had luck,
missed what we all would duck
if we'd the choice: feeling iller and iller.
Long live the instant killer!

Sestina: The Literary Gathering

At one end of the peculiar table Jeremy
sat, and talked about poetry to Carl.
He was a bit of a nutter. Next to him, Sheila
was eating a farinaceous dish. Lewis
listened intently to the words of Ursula.
They were all drinking cider. And so was Jane.

There was something quiet and achieved about Jane –
of course she was a good deal older than Lewis –
and she hadn't got the manic quality of Jeremy
nor did she understand engineering, like Carl,
Or the details of catering, which obviously Ursula
had at her fingertips. They all liked Sheila.

They all agreed there was no one like Sheila
for lovability. Music to Jeremy
was the breath of life. Often, to Carl,
he would play his autoharp – this delighted Ursula
and certainly caused some pleasure to Jane –
sitting in the meadow with the cows and Lewis.

'Lewis?' said Jane. 'He's a dark horse, Lewis!'
'You never know what he's thinking!' cried Sheila.

'He's a very nice boy' was the verdict of Ursula;
he seemed more ordinary to Carl and Jeremy.
He was fond of Milton (he once told Jane) –
but only modern poets appealed to Carl.

There was a hint of dark Satanic mills about Carl,
a contained intelligence; no fly-by-night Jeremy,
he hadn't the open character of Ursula,
in this respect he was more like Jane
or the sheep and the cattle. And only Sheila
seemed to understand him – except for Ursula.

There was a bardic bravery about Ursula.
Not even Lewis, or Jane, or Sheila
had her bravura – in the words of Lewis
'She is the mother of us all!' For Jane
Ursula's writing was the tops, and Carl
confessed he was staggered, and even Jeremy,

though he liked Carl and respected Jane
and admired Lewis (and the work of Sheila),
said how he, Jeremy, really worshipped Ursula.

Every Doggerel has its Day

The sun winks back from the back of the blade – John Arlott, BBC
commentary on the Second Test Match, England v. Australia,
11 July 1977

The sun winks back from the back of the blade,
the commentators sit in the shade
and, however many runs are made,

it's a funny old game – sentimental too,
a ritual practised for me and you –
and Youth is the cause of the hullabaloo.

When the arm is strong and the eye is keen
the idea of old age is quite obscene.
But the County Cap (and the might-have-been)

lose the throwing arm and the timing sense,
however clever, however dense,
and the past, at last, is the only tense –

even the legendary W. G. Grace
at the very end couldn't stand the pace.
He vanished too – though not without trace –

and even a batsman as great as Hobbs
when he lay dead couldn't handle lobs –
this is what causes our sighs and sobs.

Old men with MCC-striped ties
lament lost vigour with watery eyes –
the active stroking of balls (and thighs).

Cricket for them's an escape from Life,
the worries of business, children, wife;
as Death stands by with his surgeon's knife

each fancies himself as a Peter Pan,
a young attractive cricketing man,
one of the fastest who ever ran

between the wickets or in to bowl,
a batsman with genius to lift the soul,
a merrier hitter than Old King Cole.

The game, as they sit and watch for hours,
reminds them of their longlost powers
until it's over – and *Send No Flowers*.

Cowardice*

Do you remember, in the Twenties,
the songs we used to sing,
reading our Westermans and Hentys, before the days of Bing?
Gramophones were very sharp and tinny,
we could sit there and applaud
shows with stars like Laddie, Sonnie, Binnie,
Jack and Jessie, June and Claude.
We had no truck with opus numbers
or anything called Art –
and fox-trots (long before the rumbas)
gave us our happy start. . . .

This was our taste/ of the future,
we embraced/ that decade,
gleaming in glamour, with our hope not betrayed.
There lay Love – which our ten-year-old scoffing
felt above (girls with men!) – in the offing.

The sight of women set us giggling,
their bottoms broad and fat,
the Charleston and that sexy wriggling,
their bosoms not so flat,
as they jumped and bumped in that gay chorus –
though we watched the dance with scorn,
this was Life cavorting there before us,
and the reason we were born.
Of this we were just dimly conscious,
uneasily we'd sit
and judge, severe, like monks with tonsures –
soon to be part of it. . . .

It was all necks/ with arms round them,
grown-up sex/ on display –
a mystery coming our way.
We weren't too frightened,

* Based on 'Dear Little Café', from Noël Coward's *Bitter Sweet*. In 1926 (for the record) I was ten years old.

we felt partly enlightened
in that faced-by-the-future far decade.

Love Song

As you get old you begin to wonder –
what was all that lightning and thunder
actually about?
It was more than holding hands,
it had a lot to do with glands –
but now you're far out,

floating calmly in a lonely seascape;
passionate rose-garden, stormed treescape
very long ago
left behind – what they call Youth
seems now ridiculous, uncouth
(if you want to know).

As you settle into peace, or dourness,
that bitter-sweet, that sweet-and-sourness,
is a vanished taste;
yet those who never clasped and kissed
don't know exactly what they missed
or what went to waste.

Afrokill

1
The striped horse
is red inside
like sliced cake
There should be a notice
LIONS AT WORK

2
Pudgy plush muzzles
of faded yellow
of teddy-bear
show pinkness
from blood-nuzzle

3
They roll over
on invisible
beds, armchairs, divans,
sleeping so
foodful

4
The demon-faced
square pack-dogs
laugh at the banquet
brown snarling
lackeys

5
Last come the hopping
horrors
with big wings,
clean wavebreak
on shipwreck ribs.

Back

They come back, the terrible old words,
words like 'heart-piercing',
from the bad poems in the anthologies,
when I hear the voices of the children playing –
but not what they are saying.

I think back, ten or eleven years,
when we could hear sing
our own kids' trebles – the tree of knowledge is
apt to grow too fast in any London garden –
and soon our feelings harden.

They float back, like an archaic rhyme,
brightly transpiercing
parental minds, strong as old theologies,
sweet, that all too soon will grow both sour and flatter –
what they're saying doesn't matter.

A Contemporary Film of Lancasters in Action

To see them bombing up
and wheeling off into the dusk,
nose to tail, queueing, turning for the take-off,
like long-jumpers each one coming up
stationary
before they begin the run before the jump,
piloted by volunteer bank clerks.
Is my emotion bogus or inflationary?

I was never a hero,
the shark's tooth, boar's tusk,
seeming less frightening than this kind of flying,
for all kinds of courage rated zero,

admiringly
I admit they did what I could never,
sleepwalkers showing a sleepless courage –
long flights to firework climax, untiringly.

Obstinate, I survive
and, writing in this summer musk,
I say they were the patient venturing lions
and I the mean dog that stayed alive;
we owe them
every valedictory mark of respect
(bravery's facing such boring dangers)
that we can possibly, too late, show them.

A 14-Year-Old Convalescent Cat in the Winter

I want him to have another living summer,
to lie in the sun and enjoy the *douceur de vivre* –
because the sun, like golden rum in a rummer,
is what makes an idle cat *un tout petit peu ivre* –

I want him to lie stretched out, contented,
revelling in the heat, his fur all dry and warm,
an Old Age Pensioner, retired, resented
by no one, and happinesses in a beelike swarm

to settle on him – postponed for another season
that last fated hateful journey to the vet
from which there is no return (and age the reason),
which must soon come – as I cannot forget.

Conversation Piece

I sit and hear my mother and my aunt
talking of dog-carts, of a century gone
I try to imagine (there are some who can't).
Their total age is 181.
Under the clothes, the bodies were the same
as those the striptease, shamelessly as cards,
deals to the watchers now. Just the same game
but played by different rules; *ripostes, on guards,*

masks of all sorts, the flirting with a fan,
a kind of fencing with an instinct. Who loved who
they had their ways of knowing, woman and man.
Something outside them told them what to do.
They weren't direct like us (are we direct?),
Victoria sat there like a monolith
but even nice girls knew what to expect,
how Zeus crept up on Leda in the myth –

without a visiting card, in fancy dress.
No lady left the house without her gloves.
Deafness makes meaning something they must guess,
arthritis stiffens Venus and her doves,
for four decades no lovemaking at all –
beauty was jolly, with a motoring veil.
There should be writing, writing on the wall:
All sex shall fail, but love shall never fail.

The Death of W. S. Gilbert at Harrow Weald

Imagine that flat glassy lake in 1911,
a very Victorian part of the prosperous house
(architect: Norman Shaw),
a beautiful hot summer's day in 1911.

'The tiny island in the middle of the lake flames with azaleas . . .
The water's edge is fringed with golden iris and forget-
   me-nots,
and beside the winding pathway there is white heather for good
   fortune.
It is all set in a greenwood carpeted with half-uncurled
   bracken ferns,
where the shadowy fading bluebells might be fancied to
   ring
a muffled peal from fairyland.'
Into that water steps the white foot of a lady
and then, perhaps more timidly, the white foot of another
   lady.
They wear commodious and decorous bathing garments.
The water is very cold.
One lady is the pupil of the other lady
on that hot summer's day in 1911.
Gilbert has had lunch at the Junior Carlton,
he is teaching the more mature lady to swim. He is 74.

'My pupil was a much better swimmer than I,
and soon outdistanced me. We were both unaware
that the lake was deep further out,
and presently she tried to touch bottom and found herself
out of her depth. She shrieked out,
"Oh, Miss Emery, I am drowning!"'

A heavy body plunges into the water
like an old bull, like the leader of the herd,
with the scrotum tightened by that cold lake of 1911.
He swims to her, shouts advice: 'Put your hands on my
   shoulders!'
She feels him sink under her. He doesn't come up.
She struggles to the bank, he is dead of heart failure.

Is there a moral for old men? *Don't fool about with ladies?*
But all the same it's good to die brave
on a beautiful hot summer's day in 1911.

The Late Eighties*

To her
I am a coloured blur,
   a just-heard voice,
   as she sits there —
she hasn't any choice.

Life fades
like on-off hearing aids,
   and in her sleep
   the realler world
is dreaming, long and deep.

This now
needs living through somehow,
   patience is all
   and the time left,
though slow, is surely small.

I touch
the body changed so much,
   she understands
   some tenderness
through bony arms and hands.

Contact
is joining and a fact;
   we once were one,
   and touching's how
all lovemaking gets done.

   * For my mother

On First Looking into Michael Grant's Cities of Vesuvius

In battledress, yes, I was there. That dramatic great wartime eruption
    spewed out the red-hot shit; it looked very splendid
                at night
crushing the villas and trees, and the ash came down, a
              red-purple,
    to the depth of an old-fashioned foot. We moved the
              trucks and the guns
for safety. But our letters home were security-minded. No
              mention.
    You needed a four-wheel drive to churn through that stuff
              on the road.
This was in March '44 (as the clubland talks would remind you),
    of Europe's one active volcano the last recorded display.
Before this happened, I took, on an outing, a party of gunners
    (we weren't operational then) to Pompeii; they wanted the
              church,
the wine-shops, the cheap souvenirs. I opted, alone, for the *Scavi*.
    I had one guide to myself – and paid with a tin of
              corned beef.
We covered a lot of the ground. His English was good but not
              perfect –
    I was pleased to hear of a king whose name seemed to be
              Charles the Turd.
Although I went there three times – with a friend on
              two visits –
    and the guide remarked with a grin, as we looked at the
              rough plaster thighs,
how it was obvious enough that the body we saw was a woman.
We went round the brothel as well. He lit up the paintings
              on walls
with a candle held high; you could see where each girl's
              speciality, pictured
    above the door of her room, enticed you inside to her skill.
He unlocked for us, too, with his key, that famous and
              frivolous fresco
    which shows the soldier who weighs his huge uncircumcised
              cock

on the scales, and the gold goes up – for pleasure's more
                                precious than money.
Behind us, by accident, there (for this is inside a house
                                door)
an American nurse walked by. She gave a great 'Oo!' and
                                fled, shaken.
I don't know what it's like now. But *Off Limits* would,
                                then, be the words;
and the delicate souls of the girls were protected, the brothel was
                                banned; though
plain enough in the road you could see a large bas-relief
                                tool
to point the vernacular way to the house dedicated to Venus.
With a naked foot, on dark nights, it must have been
                                useful, at that.
Herculaneum wasn't so good. The best thing of all was
                                the statue
that shows Pan at work on a goat. This was our verdict, at
                                least.

So, Grant, you swim into my ken. With your writing, so large
                                and clear, telling
of thirty-three years ago now – more or less, give or take,
                                to the day
when the boil on the neck of the land burst, on the warlike
                                eighteenth
and we stood with our drinks, there, to watch, on the roof
                                of the officers' mess,
how the lava rolled down in the dark, a slow raw mass on
                                the skyline.
We didn't think so much, then, of the suffering; how those
                                who died
choked in the chemical fumes – like the brave and inquisitive
                                Pliny,
like the dog at the end of its chain. That's one of the things
                                about war.
The dying was commonplace, then. It was interesting, more
                                than distressing.
And of course you're entirely right, the gladiatorial shows
were disgusting (as Seneca said); more so than the drinking and
                                fucking.

99

Dr Arnold, the father, who wrote that the Bay of Naples
                                    was one
long drama (and 'fearsome' too) of Sin and Death, and, yes,
                                    Pleasure,
    got it wrong in his Puritan way – and so did his talented
                                    son.
Why should there be shame? No one lived (as you say) to be
                           much over forty –
    over most of the world, to this day, that's an average life.

We are exceptions, aloof and well-dressed in our self-conscious
                                    cities.
    If any small British town, perhaps a resort like Torquay,
were quickly hermetically sealed, volcanoed and covered
                        for ever,
    would archaeologists find such a high standard of art?
Architecture, as well. I think you make a good point there.
    I know they crucified slaves. There was cruelty, but
                        easiness too;
the easiness of a land where the passions could be quite volcanic
    but with the blue sea and sky there was always benevolent
                                      sun.

The Moment

There are even photographs of it:
the moment when, for the first time,
in that tense, expectant landscape,
the enemy troops appear.

There they are, advancing –
Germans from World War One
running with rifles.
As, from far back in time, so many others.

You are the opposing infantry –
this means you.
Your brain falters. *This
is it*, you think,

*these are the ones we've heard
so much about.* Like old people
when, for the first time, they confront
the unambiguous symptoms.

Pian dei Giullari

Never go back, they say. Never go back.
I went back.

With my twenty-one-year-old daughter
I walked through the Porta Romana,
up the Erta Canina,
round the curved Giramonte
and high beyond the city.

I was twice as old as then.
A lot of it I didn't recognize,

I thought we were lost —
till a name startled me into recognition:
Pian dei Giullari.
A small hilly road
but there, as in sentimental dreams,
was the straight drive through the olive orchard,
the house in faded orange with barred windows,
our once Headquarters.

And there, almost opposite,
the entrance to her villa
where 28 embraced 16.

Was this sad or happy?

Our weak, nice Major died
(I saw his obituary by accident),
the love affair came to nothing.

In those days we were careless —
as the war was careless of us.
Nobody thought very far ahead.
Girls were like wine for the drinking.

The landscape that we saw from our windows
in a time of cicadas and nightingales
stood there unaltered.
I looked at it and felt the warm lightness
of khaki drill on my shoulders.

'And Female Smells in Shuttered Rooms'

Short square fingers stuffing pipes
and Kilpeck witches in the streets,
all the Apeneck Sweeney types
riding women, staining sheets!

Sensitives wince into the world,
it seems to them so rough and coarse;
French poets, filigreed and pearled,
are better than a winged horse

and perfumes floating round an arm
than the crude odours of the groin –
foul Circe with her porcine charm
and Charon with his deadly coin!

★　★　★

Once, Eliot, I was shy as you
and impotent as you (I guess);
I failed at what I tried to do,
my sex-life was an awful mess.

But Stephen, Wystan, Christopher
enjoyed themselves with loads of boys,
they did not hesitate, demur,
or shrink from treating them like toys.

The lad is sad who masturbates.
It's good but not quite good enough –
though (once) was good enough for Yeats.
The wet warmth of that furry muff,

the girlish kiss, attracted still,
tiptilted tits, the big-eyed gaze –
I ended feeling rather ill;
I missed my homosexual phase.

A forest, round about, of cocks
grew up, a sexual Sacred Wood,

to flaunt Eternity, mock clocks;
and there, alone, I weeping stood.

Those others kicked the gong around –
Tom, Dick (especially Dick) and Harry
gave them the bliss I never found.
They even took time off to marry.

A nightmare (you could call it) and
the worse because I was so young –
Love seemed a Never Never Land.
Like Keats, infected in the lung,

I yearned for Light that never was
(there's not much fun in lonely yearning)
and this was made much worse because
I wasn't in a job and earning.

So unemployed and unenjoyed,
I sipped my bitter, loveless cup –
until, like Fathers out of Freud,
the bloody Army took me up!

Sonnet: The Greedy Man Considers Nuclear War

I suppose you all realize we shall lose the sizzling sausages
and the mild mountains of mashed potatoes!
Boiled silverside with dumplings, raspberries and cream!
We shall vanish from the pecking order of the tikka chicken,
trout with almonds will swim away from us,
little lambs no more will jump into our mouths,
fragrant with rosemary; all the good wholesome food
will vanish just as surely as sophisticated dishes!

And what shall we be left with? Some assorted politicians
not very good to eat, some dispirited root crops,

tinned food perhaps – everything else burned up,
the culture of the kitchen, the chef's wisdom of the ages
vanished in a flame like the bread in a toaster!
The end of eating civilization as we know it!

Jubilate Matteo

For I rejoice in my cat Matty.
For his coat is variegated in black and brown, with white
    undersides.
For in every way his whiskers are marvellous.
For he resists the Devil and is completely neuter.
For he sleeps and washes himself and walks warily in the ways of
    Putney.
For he is at home in the whole district of SW15.
For in this district the great Yorkshire Murderer ate his last meal
    before he entered into captivity.
For in the Book of Crime there is no name like John Reginald
    Halliday Christie.
For Yorkshire indeed excels in all things, as Geoffrey Boycott is
    the best Batsman.
For the Yorkshire Ripper and the Hull Arsonist have their horns
    exalted in glory.
For Yorkshire is therefore acknowledged the greatest County.
For Hull was once of the company, that is now of Humberside.
For Sir Leonard Hutton once scored 364 runs in a Test Match.
For Fred Trueman too is a flagrant glory to Yorkshire.
For my cat wanders in the ways of the angels of Yorkshire.
For in his soul God has shown him a remarkable vision of
    Putney.
For he has also trodden in the paths of the newly fashionable.
For those who live in Gwendolen Avenue cry 'Drop dead,
    darling!'
For in Cambalt Road and Dealtry Road where the Vet lives
    there are professional people.
For Erpingham Road and Danemere Street and Dryburgh Road
    include the intelligentsia.

For in Clarendon Drive the British Broadcasting Corporation is rampant.
For the glory of God has deserted the simple.
For the old who gossiped in Bangalore Road are unknown to the dayspring.
For there is a shortage of the old people who adorned the novels of William Trevor.
For in the knowledge of this I cling to the old folkways of Gwalior Road and Olivette Street.
For I rejoice in my cat, who has the true spirit of Putney.

The Meeting

In the long and boring meeting,
in the hot and boring meeting,
there was shouting by the Chairman,
bullying almost by the Chairman,
people rose on points of order,
caused chaos with points of order,
argument became emotive,
all the words used were emotive,
and this was the obvious reason
passion overcame all reason.

Everything was twice repeated,
sometimes more than twice repeated,
as they worked through the agenda
(it seemed elastic, that agenda,
becoming longer, never shorter),
their utterances grew long, not shorter,
it was just like spreading butter,
words went further, like spread butter,
covering each subject thinly,
covering almost nothing thinly.

People talked about resigning,
disgruntled talk was of resigning,

accusations in a covey
flew like partridge in a covey,
yet this was not entertaining –
it sounds like drama, entertaining
as the TV scenes in courtrooms –
this was *not* like scenes in courtrooms,
it contrived to be quite boring,
really quite immensely boring.

It was more like scenes where children
shout insults at other children,
it was like a verbal punch-up,
more long-winded than a punch-up,
but the bitterness and anger
brought out words like knives in anger,
it was more like verbal murder
if there's boredom in a murder –
any moderate survivors
in the end *felt* like survivors.

Like being rescued from a snowstorm,
or blinding words whirled like a snowstorm;
they could only cry for brandy,
go to pubs and order brandy,
they felt they deserved some medals
like the Army's campaign medals –
through the tumult and the shouting
(quiet was strange after the shouting)
they achieved the peace of something
through the meeting – which was something.

It was like peace after beating
heads on walls, like hours of beating
heads on walls and never stopping –
till at last the joy of stopping
seemed a truly great achievement,
lack of pain, a great achievement,
it's so lovely when you stop it!
Negative delight, to stop it,
flooded through them after meeting
at that long hot boring meeting!

A Ballad of the Good Lord Baden-Powell

(Companion piece to Lawrence Durrell's 'Ballad Of The Good Lord Nelson')

If Lord Baden-Powell ever had a stand,
sex in the head or sex in the hand,
he fixed his mind on Matabeleland
      (till he pumped it all into a Lady)

He hadn't heard about white slave trafficking,
the only relief he had was Mafeking,
he liked war and the crying and havocking
      (till he jumped it all into a Lady)

He was a virgin who married late,
he told all the lads not to masturbate,
of blindness and madness this could create
      (till he bumped it all into a Lady)

In *Scouting For Boys* he clearly said
if temptation raises its ugly head
don't sleep in too warm or soft a bed
      (till he lumped it all into a Lady)

Never, he said, play fast and loose
with the pure male fluid, it's a vital juice –
cold baths will save you from self-abuse
      (till he flumped it all into a Lady)

On Brownsea Island the first Boy Scouts
were quite as green as Brussels Sprouts
and tied in knots by love's ins and outs
      (yes, he humped it all into a Lady)

But Puritans marry and fall in love,
Venus can coo like a well-born dove
and love is below as well as above
      (how he clumped it all into a Lady!)

When he wrote *Rovering To Success*
he'd seen a woman without a dress –
which once he would have thought sheer wickedness
    (and he rumped it all into a Lady)

So now his Gospel for ever abides,
proof against changing times and tides,
it's plainly written: *Boy scouts, girl guides*
    (wow! he dumped it all into a Lady!)

Burlesque: Auden in the Forties

Deftly, admiral, from your fly
  Draw the huge unwilling cock,
Let unlettered lovers sigh,
  Love can fade and time can mock,
But you are Venus' prey
    From head to toe
And twice as gay
    As any well-hung, bell-bottomed
    Matelot.

'Hello, sailor!' is the cry
  History greets you with in bars,
The pink cadets scream 'Me, oh My!'
  While mad Furies in fast cars
Drive past but not away,
    Whatever you
May think or say,
    They're ready, hell or high water,
    To pursue.

Barbarians drink castles dry,
  Darlings live and die in bed,
All our futures are a lie,
  Truth invests the past instead:
Pretty blossoms on the may,

        Louche blackbirds urge
You not to stay –
        The fateful poem, well-written,
    Is a dirge.

They Flee from Me That Sometime Did Me Seek

At this moment in time
the chicks that went for me
in a big way
are opting out;
as of now, it's an all-change situation.

The scenario was once,
for me, 100% better.
Kissing her was viable
in a nude or semi-nude situation.
It was *How's about it, baby?*,
her embraces were relevant
and life-enhancing.

I was not hallucinating.
But with regard to that one
my permissiveness
has landed me in a forsaking situation.
The affair is no longer on-going.
She can, as of now, explore new parameters –
How's about it? indeed!
I feel emotionally underprivileged.
What a bitch!
(and that's meaningful!).

Crucifixion

Suppose they came along one morning and said 'Right!
To-day we're going to crucify you!' It would come as a
shock, to say the least; and particularly if they had already
set up a brand new wooden cross, handmade, in your
back garden, and had the hammers and high quality nails
ready, no expense spared, to do the thing in style. After
the first numbness of the shock, who would be able to
resist shouting and screaming, completely hysterical or
even technically mad? There would certainly be fainting
and falling about. We forget too easily how such cruelty
was once commonplace, no more regarded than
(nowadays) a starving lost dog in the harsh streets of a big
city. The man or woman who could contemplate the
endurance of such torture – for they would not hesitate to
crucify women, and even children – with the calm and
philosophical courage advised by the Ancients would be
rare indeed.

A Pindaric Ode on the Occasion of the Third Test Match Between England and Australia, Played at Headingley, – 16–21 July, 1981

Well, GATTING was batting and YALLOP came in at a gallop to save
a single . . . we could mix and mingle with the loud crowd, on our
telescreens we saw the best match ever to be called a Test Match . . .

Don't be abrupt, don't interrupt,
just keep quiet, don't riot, sit still and listen,
hear the Umpires' bell – I'm ready to tell
a story of glory and the unfading laurel crowns that glisten . . .

THURSDAY
Australia went in first, they were soon grinding away on a day
when England were finding it hard. I tell you, mate,

the English bowlers didn't bowl very straight,
it was like watching a coffee-grinder or standing
behind a cement-mixer, as those batsmen went
through the motions, they knew they had oceans of time. Their
    slowness was a crime
and didn't produce standing ovations – but justified,
buildings don't stand up without foundations . . .

FRIDAY
203 for 3, and a catch dropped by GOWER, the power
and the glory seemed as though it had really deserted BREARLEY.
OLD bowled quite well; but all this day
the Australians seemed well on their way.
DYSON didn't charge at the ball like a bison;
but he made 102, and 102s, like the 89 made by HUGHES,
    and YALLOP'S 58, meant a good score – and a lot more.
    Confidence.
They declared at 9 for 401 – for England not much fun, though
    BOTHAM bowled straight and moved the ball both early
    and late,
the one ray of light in the gloom (6 for 95). Still, England's
    doom
could be seen to loom. BOTHAM seemed to prove it –
if he could swing it, the Australians too would certainly move it,
by seam and flight.
But no untoward fright. No English wicket fell that night.

SATURDAY
Yet England didn't rise again on that third day.
GOOCH out for 2. The thing to do seemed to be to
mooch around, BOYCOTT 12, BREARLEY 10, even
GOWER only very briefly came into flower.
24. Again some light from BOTHAM – where others were thrifty
he was prodigal, with a well-struck 50.
LILLEE, ALDERMAN, LAWSON bowled well – at the stumps.
Far better than the English bowlers. A bad night, with grinding
    molars
and all England's supporters down in the dumps.

MONDAY
England 174 all out and, following on,

GOOCH, with the score at zero, had already gone.
The radio mentioned odds of 500 to 1
for an England win. But this wasn't the Oval, there weren't any
   LAKERS,
and, with regard to these odds, there can't have been
   many takers.
Would Australia even have to bat again?
The most sensible thing seemed to be to pray for rain.
227 to avoid the innings defeat.
BOYCOTT played straight, calm and unflappable (46),
some of WILLEY'S more aggressive strokes (33) were very
   clappable.
But 4 down for 41! Even 5 for 105,
there didn't seem much to keep our hopes alive.
It was like the tide inexorably flooding in over the sand,
seven wickets had gone for 135. No sign of a stand,
like King Canute, nobody could send the sea back with a
   cricket boot,
92 runs still needed for Australia to bat again, the steep hill of
   the follow-on
and only three wickets left,
any English laugh must have been a hollow one!

But BOTHAM, looking like a lion on a British egg,
seemed to be willing to have a brief, glorious thrash,
pulling, driving, cutting and sweeping to leg,
with (once) something not much different from a tennis
   overhead smash . . .

and, slowly but surely, we realized that he knew what he
   was doing
and although it was very clear that he was riding his luck
the ball met the meat of the bat, this wasn't just cause for booing
or irresponsible (like the slogger who's out for a duck).

The next day's papers compared him to
that six-hitting fabulous Croucher, Jessop –
and indeed he jumped down the pitch like a gressop
(the Old English for what James Joyce with his Irish voice called
   a gracehoper
and most ordinary people call a grasshopper).

One particular six, a tremendous one, parabola-tall,
made one feel pretty sorry for the ball.

DILLEY, too, turned aggressive. 56 runs, and all made with style.
Someone shouted 'Why didn't you bowl like that?'
He was out at 252. A century partnership.
The Australian bowlers; even LILLEE, began to look ordinary.
BOTHAM's hundred. BREARLEY gave him the *stay there!* signal,
    very clearly.
From then on he shielded OLD, running singles at the ends
    of overs
and scoring in fours only (twos were difficult).
OLD was bowled for 29, a good innings.
Then it was WILLIS. 351 for nine
at close of play. Fine. A commentator was heard to say:
'They need a hundred runs to bowl at!' These they had.
It still looked hopeless, but not quite so bad.

TUESDAY
BOTHAM hit one more four, ALDERMAN got WILLIS.
356 all out. When they went in
Australia needed only 130 to win.
It all went quietly ahead, though BOTHAM got WOOD for ten.
DYSON and CHAPPELL looked as firm as rocks, and then
DILLEY went off to have a boot repaired. WILLIS took over –
and from then on the Australian batsmen were never in clover.
That wild Goose flew in like a bat out of Hell –
3 wickets in 11 balls, without a run being scored!
Surely the batsmen to come must have prayed to the Lord!
CHAPPELL, HUGHES and YALLOP – the names say it all.
This was the kind of bowling you can't play at all!
OLD had BORDER for a duck. MARSH didn't have BOTHAM's luck
and DILLEY boundary-caught him at fine leg, one of the hardest
    blows struck.
Before that DYSON went. 68 for 6. Soon just 75 for 8.
Only LILLEE at the end, with BRIGHT, showed any kind of fight.
BRIGHT 19, LILLEE 17 (DYSON made 34
and this was very easily the top score).
55 runs needed. Two wickets to fall.
WILLIS had LILLEE caught by GATTING, a mishit hook off a less
    straight ball.

114

BREARLEY said afterwards, in a sort of magnificat,
'I didn't think WILLIS could still bowl like that.'

BOTHAM came back. OLD dropped ALDERMAN twice in an over.
If that had been FLETCHER
that Yorkshire Chauvinist crowd would have made a meal of it,
    you betcher
life, as one of the commentators said.
Still, though everyone was tense, under his beard
OLD'S face must have been a bit red . . .

Finally, though, WILLIS knocked out BRIGHT'S middle stump,
and everyone jumped for joy, a really
unbelievable jump!
111 all out. They'd done it by 18 runs . . .
And this is an ode to Cricket, Cricket and its white-robed sons!
Like the bounce of a rugger ball, you can't tell which way it'll
    go,
it's totally unpredictable, if it's like anything it's at all
it's truly like a game of soccer played with a rugger ball!
But of course you must praise WILLIS (8 for 43)
and BOTHAM'S magnificent innings – 149 not out.
Goose and Guy the Gorilla
were the two favourite flavours, like (say) Strawberry and
    Vanilla –
but MIKE BREARLEY also deserves praise,
as a first-class Captain in a good many different ways.

This tribute that mangles the epic and the lyric,
this rough populist Pindaric panegyric,
this dithyrambic doggerel is here to make the claim
that since STODDARD did it in Sydney in 1894
no other Test side in history has ever followed on and still won
    the game!

A Bit Of A Ballad

(Scotland v. Australia, Murrayfield, 18 December 1981)

Oh, broken, broken was the play!
And blawn the half-time whistle!
The Wallabies hae scored tries three,
Four penalties the Thistle.

The second half now gars begin,
On the snaw-stripit green,
And but twelve points the braw Scots hae,
The Wallabies fifteen.

But 'tis the bonny Andy Irvine
That kicks the penalty
That levels a', 15–15,
As level as your e'e.

And they hae ta'en the whisky malt
That stand to see the battle,
And syne they harry the Scottish team,
As drovers harry cattle!

The lions on the standards roar,
And Scotland scores again!
'Tis the muckle Rutherford –
A drappit goal, ye may ken!

'Hauld fast! Hauld fast!' Clerk Irvine cries,
'My bonny lads, wi' me!
We'll weill withstand, on either hand,
The assaults o' the enemie!'

The Wallabies are ravenous,
They sling the ba' aboot –
The Scots defence stands firm as rock,
They dinna care a hoot!

There's but five minutes' playing time,
Australians leap and rin,

116

And 'tis gowd jerseys everywhere,
Like a rugby loony-bin!

But 'tis the muckle Rutherford
Has ta'en the ba' in's hands
And kicked it full high i' the freezing air
And higher than the stands.

The ba' has landed on its point,
The ba' has bounced full high –
And 'tis the wee Renwick has caught it and
'Tis an inescapable try!

Oh, wae, wae, were the Wallabies,
Baith here and owre the faem,
Tae see the braw wee Renwick rin
And bear the victory hame!

For now 'tis 15–22 –
Australia does trail,
A score that hurts. Irvine converts,
Like driving in a nail!

And so rejoice in Embro toun,
The final whistle blaws,
Mak merrie, 24–15!
All Scots, they hae guid cause!

Singable

Maimed personalities make the best poets still,
with flaws all over the shop,
opium and alcohol, no one could say of them
they never touched a drop –
and there's a strain of reclusive old ladies too
who hardly go out to tea,
agoraphobes, with a murderous loneliness –
not jolly, like you and me –

all the neurotics, the Muse will quite welcome them,
yes, *and* their queerness and quirks,
what does it matter? It turns out so singable,
it doesn't gum up the works!

Aros Castle

I first saw Aros Castle when I was ten, in 1926 –
a ruin with a great ruined window like an eye.
My father took me shooting rabbits. I can fix

all that in my mind. There was a man with a ferret,
the rabbits lived under the rocks, quite near the shore.
I shot my first-ever rabbit. I was proud with acquired merit.

And on the small headland the Castle sat still,
looking like a picture postcard view from a window.
After that summer I didn't see it again until

I came to Mull in 1937 (I was twenty-one),
I was reading *Present Indicative*, I'd just finished Cambridge,
I had no job in prospect, a lot remained to be done,

it was hot and we drove Margery's car round the island roads,
Calgary, Gribun and so on, a lovely summer,
and the Castle still sat there like something with loads
of time on its hands. The eye never blinked or shifted.
It stood there clear. If it vanished, it would come back –
as soon as the rain stopped or the mist lifted.

When (in 1967?) I saw it again
I had Margo with me, it was Easter,
a huge rabbit popped up and eyed us with disdain

outside the window, at breakfast. The world had carried
on with its wars and its worries, the Castle notwithstanding,
and I had been eleven years married.

That eye never closed. It wasn't designed for sleeping.
It seemed (perhaps this is the pathetic fallacy)
as though it had Time or something in its own safe keeping.

In 1968 we brought the kids before its unchanging face.
Jane had to dive into Tobermory Bay from a boat
among a lot of jellyfish. It was part of a race.

And this year, 1981, was (so far) the last time.
I once walked to the Castle – its base is smothered in nettles
and walking round it isn't much of a pastime.

I think it's nearly 500 years old, but I might be wrong.
Obviously someone once took trouble to destroy it –
it's a long time since, as a castle, it was really on song!

Man and boy, you might say, I've been there and seen it,
as tourist and time-traveller. If they holocaust us
(if Reagan and the Russians really mean it)
I bet that crumbling picturesque dump outlasts us!
Meanwhile it's into thoughtfulness, if not depression,
that that non-seeing picture postcard eye creepily casts us.

The Good Companions

They stand behind you and whisper:
Fill your glass! and *Fill your plate!*
Now they are nameless, but later you'll know their names,
fiends and familiars with eating and drinking games:
Big Belly and Red Nose and Brain Damage.
They'll find you, sure as fate!

Tip-tankards, they jog the elbow:
Let's finish it! Have the other half!
They'll be your companions throughout your later life,
the Knights of the Blissful Bottle, the Knavish Knife,

Lord Blood Pressure, Lady Redvein-Cheeknet,
the lewd litre, the loud laugh!

I could do with a drink! they whisper,
Oh, for a knife! Oh, for a fork!
Though they're refined gourmets and eat a lot of French
you'll know them by a very piglike kind of stench,
Lady Burper, Bad Breath, Fartwell —
all dying for the popping of a cork!

Robert Graves

When Robert Graves got involved
with a wildly unsuitable woman
his problems were *not* solved —

though he, later, did get married
to a much more suitable woman.
But he was considerably harried.

by an arrogant arid virago —
a madly unsuitable woman.
If he'd sailed off in an Argo

like Jason, and left them all screaming
(each clearly unsuitable woman),
it might have been better — but dreaming

of Goddesses (White) and of Muses
(the *younger* unsuitable woman)
is what the male masochist chooses!

O Governesses and O Nurses!
From the strains of Unsuitable Women
came the excellence of his verses!

I.M. Anthony Blunt

ob. 26 March 1983 Portsea Hall, Paddington

They took your body, in its coffin, to a battered whitish van,
    quite plain,
from the flat that held the Poussin. Only classic Poussin can,
    unstirred,
    remain
quite so classically unaltered by the fate of mortal man –
    no word
    of pain

ever shakes the dancing shepherds or the clear blue summer sky.
    It's sad
you were shaken by a maverick clever buccaneer like Guy.
    You had,
in one sense, a lot of genuine pressing thirties reason-why.
    Good, bad,

who should say, who saw the Fascists creeping up the 'Europe'
    map?
    Dead? Red?
Both together not unusual! Hitler was the kind of chap,
    some said,
who stopped commies. Race against time! And the last
    important lap!
    He *led*!

Pressmen, who would sell their mothers for a front-page
    story's sake,
    howled loud,
threw your fox-name (it was easy, just a piece of Fleet
    Street cake)
    to the vast
    hound-crowd.
I remember charm and knowledge, wit too – *that* was
    never fake –
    time past
    allowed.

Into History

Marched eighty miles in five days; crossed a river.
We were going to cross, they said, another river – but
the nearest crossing was blocked by their 6000.
For five days, and hungry, we marched the river bank,
the enemy keeping pace on the northern side.
On the sixth, a forced march across a plain,
we got ahead; two damaged causeways, hasty sappering,
and we were over.

Two hundred miles or more in twelve starved days.

October 20. Scarcely a day's scarce rest.
October 21. Marched eighteen miles;
the next three days, another fifty-three.
Three marches more, they said, and we'd be safe –
the port, and home.

October 24, late in the day, the scouts came back.
Enemy ahead, they said, deploying for battle.

That night round a little village, clustering in,
ate skimpy rations, confessed sins, heard Mass,
and armed for battle.

At first light, knights and archers out.
A thousand yards ahead, across the field,
we saw the enemy, between the eachside woods,
stand or sit idle, breakfasting, with jokes,
some getting fighting-drunk (*our* wine was small!) –
such confidence in numbers, vast superiority.
The archers dug in stakes for cavalry.

Three or four hours of waiting, worst of all.
Cold muddy ploughland, sown with winter wheat.
So short of food nine days, nuts and berries
the archers' feeding. Rainwet and cold,
stood in our ranks, many with diarrhoea

but anchored there, mail leggings laced to plate armour,
foul with discomfort.

The order to advance. We stumbled slow and cold
over ploughed ridges. And into History . . .

NOTE   *See the account of the Battle of Agincourt (1415) in The Face of Battle by
John Keegan.*

The Falklands, 1982

This must have been more like the Boer War
than anything seen in our lifetime,
with the troopships and the cheering,
the happy homecoming, the sweetheart-and-wifetime,
everything looking over and solved,
and no civilians involved –

except a few stewardesses, Chinese in the galleys
almost by accident taken
willy-nilly on The Great Adventure,
where the Argentine fusing of the shells was often mistaken –
lucky for each floating sitting duck.
Oh yes, we had luck!

Luck that the slaughtered World War I soldiers
who died on the Somme and at Arras
would have welcomed, in their dismal trenches –
though that's not to belittle the victory of the Paras,
who lost, all in all, very few dead,
good men, well led.

At home, indeed, it was terribly like the World Cup,
though far less bright, commentated, stagey,

security making the war news nil, mostly,
but good value when they finally stopped being cagey.
Was the *General Belgrano* really offside?
A few hundred died.

And the outstanding achievements of the great Press,
particularly that section called 'yellow',
that wrote 'Up yours!' on missiles, went berserk
and shouted 'GOTCHA!' in a giant coward's bellow –
and circulation rises, like *The Sun*.
But was it well done?

Kipling's 'Recessional' told us to beware of Hubris,
and not give way to flag-waving
(they don't in the Lebanon, or Northern Ireland) –
if men's lives are worth giving, they're also worth saving.
Who let them start the bloody thing?
That's the question, there's the sting.

Sonnet: Pepys in 1660

Everybody is openly drinking the King's health!
The King is about to be back! There are bonefires everywhere!
Stable government, King and Parliament, not Cromwell's
        wobbly son!
Yet Pepys, at sixteen, saw with satisfaction the King's
        beheading.
'There's a Divinity doth hedge a King,
rough-hew him how we will!' – Samuel Butler's joke.
Charles II promises a free pardon,
proceedings only against those named by Parliament.

As you read, you can see what is coming.
Exhumation and gibbeting of regicides –
hanging, drawing and quartering for those still living.
We are still in the century when Shakespeare died,

where the racks and the fires were not thought barbaric . . .
with Pepys, his music, his ideas of order, a civilized man.

NOTE   20 October 1660 'I saw the limbs of some of our new Traytors set upon Aldersgate, which was a sad sight to see; and a bloody week this and the last have been, there being ten hanged, drawn, and quartered.'

Samuel Pepys, Diary

Sonnet: Supernatural Beings

You can't ever imagine the Virgin Mary having vulvitis or
    thrush –
she's not a real woman, she's a supernatural being,
not like the real women who are snoring and farting.
Aldous Huxley in an essay said that the angels
painted so often in Italian pictures
would need huge pectoral muscles if they were ever to fly . . .
But angels, like the Virgin, are supernatural beings.
It's all done by magic. If you can, you believe it.

And not so much *if you can*, more *if you want to* –
if you want to imagine something a bit kinder than people,
full of love and bursting with benevolence,
you go for these smiling supernatural do-gooders
that look a little patronizing to an ordinary man
and still can't prevent you getting cancer or a cold.

A Pilgrimage

W. H. Auden (1907–73)

Wystan Hugh Auden, poet, was born in this house on the 21st
February 1907 – *inscription on 54 Bootham, York*

*Max: By the way, I forgot to tell you. There's one possible
       I saw yesterday, Mrs Stagg – the wife of the
       under-manager at Windyacre Mine. We might do
       worse. Vegery gegoegod bust.*
Ceslaus: Tegight cegunt?
Max: I should think so. Her mouth's small enough, anyway.
                           – Fragment from *The Enemies of a Bishop*,
                             unpublished play by Auden and Isherwood

Before you know quite where you are
you're standing there by Bootham Bar,
with handsome houses,
a now degraded road that feeds
traffic to Harrogate and Leeds,
a school that rouses

memories of one Cambridge friend.*
A.'s beginning is my end.
He started here,
Constance Rosalie gave out
a poet who was like a shout
and far and near

we clustered round to hear the Word
as clergymen ancestors deferred
to his new genius.
He put the thirties in their place,
Life hardly dared to show its face,
while like gardenias

the lovely images were strown
in careless verses, quite full-blown,

* Frank Thistlethwaite, once at Bootham's School. The Auden house is now
one of the school buildings.

bright in what's darker,
yet doomed, though serious and select,
to feel the Dracula Effect,
like Minna Harker.

The trouble of those old decades
before the telly and Teasmades!
He told of madness
deep in the body politic
(so right, though he himself was sick)
and all our sadness

whiffled down through those sensuous lines
where Western Decadence declines –
though, to speak truly,
much D.H. Lawrence nonsense too
was there to urge both me and you
to be unruly,

obey a Leader and take vows
while lovely women, those poor cows,
stayed strict at home.
(He made a U-turn of a sort
and finally came into port
not far from Rome.)

He was engaged once, married too,
and had a girlfriend he could screw,
but all his joys
lay in the arms of flaunting Chester
(a most notorious butch-molester)
and various boys.

Osborne and Carpenter declare
such doings as would raise the hair
on heads of Mormons –
if any lad has a wet dream
they beat him, naked, pray and scream –
what a performance!

He certainly gulped sex like food,
quite the reverse of any prude,
and, wholly greedy,
he wolfed huge helpings that he carved –
his cock was never stinted, starved,
or poor and needy.

That limestone landscape and those holes,
the lead mines that could save our souls –
a feminine body
and Mother's too, it seems to me.
There's not much else that it could be.
And, cute as Noddy,

he loved them and was never irked
although those mines were now not worked –
Dad's lust, I think,
was over, there was Mum, serene
and *his*; as though Dad hadn't been!
and with the ink

he poured such symbols, partly known,
into the poems. We should clone
not Dons or Wardens
but such eccentric bards as these
and make our bookish bread and cheese
from Wystan Audens.

Rugger Song: *The Balls of the Beaver*

(Tune: 'Caviare Comes from the Virgin Sturgeon')

Castorium helpyth ayenst many Syknesses.

— Trevisa (1398)

The valuable drug Castoreum is taken from the inguinal glands of these animals. The antients had a notion it was lodged in the testicles, and that the animal, when hard pressed, would bite them off, and leave them to its pursuers, as if conscious of what they wanted to destroy him for.

— Pennant *History of Quadrupeds* (1781)

Castoreum comes from the balls of the Beaver —
Balls of the Beaver — very fine stuff!
A Beaver is truly a gay deceiver —
And often found in a lady's muff!

Beleaguered Beavers will bite their balls off —
In that confusion they escape —
Huntsman checks his hunting — calls off
All that rowdiness and rape!

Now, I'm quite glad I'm not a Beaver —
Virile value's bad, you see!
It's my girlfriend — I can't leave her —
If I did a Beaver — she'd leave me!

Love in a Valley*

Valkyrie's Valspeak in Awesome Valhalla

I used to think Wotan was vicious
in all that gear, a real soc, a mega hunk.

We flew high, a bitchen sesh,
it was radical!

Those pointy things on his helmet
were truly gnarly, the Heinies were
tubular.
And the Lowies.

Totally!

The bud was caj
we scarfed out. It was hot.
He maxed OK

OK!
How come he get so gross?
such a zod, so nerdy?
a shanky spaz?

OK!
Now I wanta say:

Gag me with a spoon!
What a geek!
You were mondo cool
but now you're grody
you make me barf
you're not buf any more . . .
Oh my God!
Kiss my tuna!
What a nerd!
Get away!
Your fat butt disgusts me!

* Spoken, as it were, by a Valley Girl in Los Angeles, living in or near the
San Fernando Valley.

Ms. Found in a Victorian Church*

Golly! Let's debag old Kingers!
What a brilliant thought!
One of our most King Size singers!
Praise him as we ought –
That would be extremely hard!
But still we'll jolly well teach him
To be a Bard!

Though we love him daily, nightly,
Calling people shags
Is the fault that very rightly
Makes him lose his bags!
To respect his fellow men –
That idea may some day reach him
And his pen!

Flying tackles are in order,
Grab him round the waist,
Hold him hard South of the Border,
Give him quite a taste
Of the fate of sods and pseuds
When they bow down and beseech him
In their feuds!

Let him know the harsh unzipping,
The outcome of the knees!
Violence is simply ripping –
Down his Y-fronts, please!
Gosh! We've got him! Chewing gum out!
In unmentionable places bleach him,
Scream and shout!

* Thought to be a poem by Sir John Betjeman about Kingsley Amis, but the presence of another hand has been suspected.

A McGonagall-type Triolet on the Full Revoltingness of Commercial Fast Food

A great double-deck of pure beef with melting cheese, pickle,
    ketchup and mustard!
Complete your meal with our crisp French Fries and a cool
    thick Shake!
Enjoy too the fried jumbo-size jumbo-tough breadcrumbed
    macho legs of the Bustard,
a great double-deck of pure beef with melting cheese, pickle,
    ketchup and mustard,
with a few lightly boiled rats' foetuses on the side, all masked in
    creamy custard!
Wash it down with a warm Guinness, topped up with
engine oil – and dunk in it our supermale Elephant Cake,
a great double-deck of pure beef with melting cheese, pickle,
    ketchup and mustard!
Complete your meal with our crisp French Fries and a cool
    thick Shake!

NOTE   *The first two lines of this poem are genuine food advertising of March 1984 in
a London take-away/eat-in restaurant.*

The Inventor of Franglais?

A Comment

*Thence to Jervas's, my mind, God forgive me, running too much after
sa fille, but elle not being within, I away by coach to the Change – and
thence home to dinner; and finding Mrs Bagwell waiting at the office
after dinner, away elle and I to a cabaret where elle and I have été
before; and there I had her company toute l'après-diner and had mon
plein plaisir of elle – but strange, to see how a woman, notwithstanding
her greatest pretences of love à son mari and religion, may be vaincue.*

– Samuel Pepys, *Diary (23 January 1665)*

Well, God, j'ai souvent pensé
(in clear or fractured français),
a pris the soul of femmes –
but toutefois the Devil maudit
is souverain of their body
and has his will of Dames!

He does all that he voulait
to each partridge or poulet,
we're instruments – c'est tout!
Bon Dieu, above, has thunder –
le Diable rules what's under –
très bon for me and you!

Les female protestations
qui annoncent their detestations
of all luxurieux men
sont for the record only,
le corps stays soft and lonely
et le fait again et again!

The Importance of Being Earnest

Jack Worthing is free, fit and fine –
and he knows about women and wine.
Less coarse than a sandbag,
he was found in a *handbag* –
on the Brighton, that famous old line.

Algy Moncrieff does a Bunbury
to places like Paris or Sunbury –
to see a sick friend
who is nearing his end –
but in truth he's at Joysville or Funbury!

There are two girls: Gwendolen, Cecily,
who go round full of wit, and quite dressily.
Lady Bracknell's the Aunt –
not her fault that it shan't
end in tears and in all ways quite messily!

C.'s governess, prune-faced Miss Prism,
Canon Chasuble; heresy, schism
fly away when *he's* there.
She'd be willing to share
any fate as his mate – cataclysm!

Now Jack's told one lie or another,
told Cecily he has a brother
called Ernest – who's wicked –
this isn't quite cricket
(no one knows yet who might be his mother).

So the Albany country-house lads –
must endure the girls' maidenly fads –
C.'s a chick who in *her* nest
wants no one not Ernest.
Ditto Gwendolen. *Christen us cads*!

is the favour they both of them ask,

it's the Canon's canonical task.
But – one last catechism –
Lady B. questions Prism,
and the Truth is revealed, with no mask!

That (how fateful and how well–arranged!)
for a *novel* the young Jack was changed
by Miss Prism, his nurse,
and for better or worse
he's the brother of Alg., long estranged!

Even better, his true given name
will revive the young Cecily's flame!
For it's Ernest (no catch!),
so it's game, set and match
(and the winner was wit in that game)!

Happiness is Girl-Shaped

(The Copywriter Sings)

You're twice as trad as Acker Bilk,
you'd be delicious
                          crumbled into milk,
there is no other of your ilk!

You're very clearly bran–enriched,
I'd like to have you
                          hedged and ditched,
no hype for you is over–pitched!

My heart, for you, has raced like Arkle,
you've got that cute
                          refreshing sparkle,
you are my light that will not darkle!

You have that tangy lemon zest,
great things have happened

on your chest,
you're way out there beyond the rest!

You make life bright and dazzling new,
you are the first
                    of precious few,
I'd like to have a private view!

You set me off like fire alarms,
persuasive as
                    a salesman's charms,
I'd make down payments on your arms!

You are the rhyme that's always true,
the whitest wash
                    that's slightly blue –
let me consume my life with you!

Rush That Bear!

There's a breathless hush over Crescent and Square
    and the Gardens are sad and still
    While everybody, yes, everywhere,
    wonders: Will
Sir John go over the hill?

The agonized cry goes up: *Rush that bear
    to his grieving, tormented side!*
    This is the comfort, in his despair,
    far and wide
all wish for him, tearful-eyed!

This is the single much-more-than-toy
    that can succour him in his need –
    Archibald, seventy years of joy,

of joy indeed,
as Venerable as Bede!

So take him by taxi, by tube or by train,
   fly him so high in the air!
   Give us some hope, let us breathe again
   (oh, if we dare!)
and speedily RUSH THAT BEAR!

NOTE In October 1983 Sir John Betjeman suffered a heart attack and his childhood teddy bear, Archibald, was brought to his hospital bed.

A Ballad Re-Creation of a Fifties Incident at Barnes Bridge

'Tis the ghost o' Colquhoun an' the ghost o' McBride
That do balcony-lean by yon auld riverside,
An' they baith are sae fou' they can scarcely see –
For they're baith at a party (where booze is free) –

An' the Sassenachs there wi' their highbrowish speech
Mak' a nebulous nectarine oot o' a peach.
But Colquhoun an' McBride hauld theirsels weil aloof,
Aye drinkin' the drinks that are ower proof.

Nae word do they speak, but they lean an' glower
Wi' the pissed perfection o' painterly power –
An' as they lean there the sun gaes doun
Like a watercolour o'er London toun,

In a' the sweet tints that the calendars love,
Wi' a braw great pink flush i' the skies above.
Och! they *do* notice this, tho' their eyes are glazed,
An' baith wi' horror are sair amazed –

Colquhoun turns tae McBride wi' a fine disgust
At the sight o' that distant an' reddenin' dust.

'Mon, but it's horrible!' 'Aye, but 'twill pass!'
An' they ply, baith, the gold, unremittin' wee glass!

NOTE   This haunting is quite a possible one, being based on an actual incident.
Colquhoun and McBride were two painters of talent from Glasgow, well-known
in the forties and fifties.

A Godly Undertaking

I continually pray for the SOU-
L of the novelist Evelyn Waugh.
It seems dark and obscure, half a MO-
LE, and unfriendly and raw.

It didn't much like fellow-ME-
N, it was snobbish and cruel to the weak,
and it harmed what he wrote with his PE
N and the words it induced him to speak.

It took sides, where it could, with the STRO-
NG and all privilege led it astray.
It's in Hell, I expect (am I WRO-
NG?) – that's why I so steadfastly pray!

The Song of the Old Soldier

Across the miles and miles of burning plain
the Army's marching, marching, and marching yet again.
Oh, yes, the fucking Army
is the terror of the land
and where the sea is wavy
you can see the sodding Navy –
but miles and miles above us,
where they can't raise a stand,
is the airy fairy Air Force with its joystick in its hand!

Across the miles and miles of frozen kelp
the Army's marching, marching, and marching without help.
Oh, yes, the fucking Army
is the terror of the girls –
there are fewer girls than gravy
for the poor old sodding Navy,
and miles and miles above us,
like the swine above the pearls,
is the airy fairy Air Force with its profile and its curls!

Across the miles and miles of mountain range
the Army's marching, marching, and marching without change.
The fearless fucking Army
leaves the babies in its wake,
while young Dan is doing Davy
in the silly sodding Navy –
but miles and miles above us,
drifting on without a brake,
is the airy fairy Air Force like a fancy piece of cake!

'The Sun' Also Rises

Oh, isn't it exciting!
There's going to be a war!!!
We hope there's lots of fighting –
we missed the one before!

Already men are drowning!
We're brave, we have no fear,
as patriots we're downing
our fearless pints of beer!

Two Harriers, one cruiser?
Our lads will put it right,
while we stay in the boozer
and carry on the fight . . .

Though we have high expenses
we shoot our mouths off quick,
large gins and their defences
are sure to do the trick!

At Death we're shouting 'Gotcha!',
we're perfect shining knights –
no diplomatic botcher
has any bleeding rights . . .

How grand for circulation
and for the Tories too,
a floor show for the Nation,
and free for me and you!

How grand for Mrs Thatcher –
she's almost out of sight!
Now Foot can never catch her,
though running day and night!

It's lovely on the telly,
home strategists agree,
when the Fascist underbelly
gets hit in time for tea!

We're full of warlike features –
and every word is priced –
despising spineless creatures
like peaceful Jesus Christ!

We know there's news in 'traitors' . . .
and as the hot war nears
like stripshow fornicators
we roar it on with cheers . . .
we hope it lasts for years!

20 May 1982

The Owl Writes a Detective Story

A stately home where doves, in dovecotes, coo –
fields where calm cattle stand and gently moo,
trim lawns where croquet is the thing to do.
This is the ship, the house party's the crew:
Lord Feudal, hunter of the lion and gnu,
whose walls display the heads of not a few,
Her Ladyship, once Ida Fortescue,
who, like his Lordship very highborn too
surveys the world with a disdainful moue.
Their son – most active with a billiard cue –
Lord Lazy (stays in bed till half past two).
A Balkan Count called Popolesceru
(an ex-Dictator waiting for a coup).
Ann Fenn, most English, modest, straight and true,
a very pretty girl without a sou.
Adrian Finkelstein, a clever Jew.
Tempest Bellairs, a beauty such as you
would only find in books like this (she'd sue
if I displayed her to the public view –
enough to say men stick to her like glue).
John Huntingdon, who's only there to woo
(a fact, except for her, the whole house knew)
Ann Fenn. And, last, the witty Cambridge Blue,

the Honourable Algy Playfair, who
shines in detection. His clear 'View halloo!'
puts murderers into a frightful stew.

But now the plot unfolds! What *déjà vu*!
There! In the snow! – The clear print of a shoe!
Tempest is late for her next rendez-vous,
Lord Feudal's blood spreads wide – red, sticky goo
on stiff white shirtfront – Lazy's billet-doux
has missed Ann Fenn, and Popolesceru
has left – without a whisper of adieu
or saying goodbye, typical *mauvais gout*!
Adrian Finkelstein, give him his due,
behaves quite well. Excitement is taboo
in this emotionless landowner's zoo.
Algy, with calm that one could misconstrue
(handling with nonchalance bits of vertu)
knows who the murderer is. He has a clue.

But who? But who? Who, who, who, who, who, who?

NOTE   This poem was written to be read aloud, and the 'oo' sounds at the
ends of the lines should be intoned like the call of an owl.

Little Ones

Folk-Hero

The one the foreign students call Ted Huge.

Negative

A landlady is not a countrywoman
A *mariage blanc* is not a white wedding
A planchette is not a ghost writer

A sperm whale is not a Don Juan
An *oeil de boeuf* is not a bullseye
A mons veneris is not the Venusberg
A peccary is not a serious sin

Creation Myth Haiku

After the First Night
the Sun kissed the Moon: 'Darling,
you were wonderful!'

The Beginning of an Augustan Ode to Masturbation, Written at the Request of Several Ladies and Gentlemen of Quality

Oh, Masturbation! Lord of Kings and Queens,
That from our Cradle bring'st us such Delight,
                    By Day and by Night
That hold'st this Realm in Thrall,
And hast so many Modes and untold Means!

A Daisychain for the Queen's Jubilee (1952–77)

Unique queendom! Mother! Renew
wives, sons, sad daughters!
So only yesterday you, undaunted,
dedicated, dominating, gave
easily your royal love endlessly,
yes, set the ethnic crown nobly
yet tremulously yours!
Simple earned devotion now will
lessen newly your real, lived,
dumb burden. Now we elevate
emotional loud delighting
garish high hymns solemnly!
Yours soundly! Yours serenely!

Note

The Daisychain was invented by my wife in the spring of 1977, when she suggested that I should write a poem where each word began with the last letter of the word before. Perhaps 'unique queendom' is stretching this rule a bit, but the principle is there.

Invasion

Is it not passing brave to be a king
and charge in arabhood through Selfridges?

Penal

The clanking and wanking of Her Majesty's prisons.

John Reginald Halliday Christie

'The same stone which the builders refused: is
become the head-stone in the corner.' – PSALM CXVIII

So the man who was once called
'Can't Do It Christie'
and 'Reggie-No-Dick'
by disappointed girls in Halifax,
rose to be the greatest sex-maniac
of his generation.

Life-Style

The farmyard squeals in the breakfast bacon

The sun is shining in the noble vintage

The eggs are clucking in the honourable omelette

The wheat is windswept in the loaves we love so

In the beefburgers the bulls are bellowing

The peat-clean water wobbles through the whisky

The calmness of cows murmurs in the milk

Two Nonsense Limericks

NONSENSE LIMERICK I

Eggwood limestone filbert horse
prayerbird angel trefoil gorse
tabard tunic
writing runic
semaphore semaphore morse!

NONSENSE LIMERICK II

Cathedral, amphetamine, string,
annuity, edelweiss, ling,
indemnity, cheese,
alabaster, demise,
ululate, underestimate, sing!

Thought About the Human Race

We are just a passing smile on the face of Venus.

Eve and the Apple

A young girl whose life-style the malicious
described, loosely, as too meretricious,
said 'When the boys peel me
and delightfully feel me,
I just feel like a Golden Delicious!'

Autumn

Life is sad and so slow and so cold
as the leaves that were green turn to gold,
as the lonely lake fills
and there's ice in the hills
and the long loathly winter takes hold . . .

Night Scene

There's a slow tolling bell in the dark
as the keepers are closing the park.
Like a desert, it's bare;
and each tree and each chair
is a blurred indeterminate mark.

Americans

Americans have very small vocabularies.
They don't understand words like 'constabularies'.
If you went up to a cop in New York and said
'I perceive you are indigenous!' he would hit you on the head.

Haiku: The Sex War

Foreskin-flensing Jews,
clitoricidal Arabs,
are locked in conflict.

Julia Wood

If Julia Wood, if only Julia Wood!
I know, by instinct, it would be so good!
If only, only, Julia, Julia Wood!

Ah, but Wood Julia? I think Julia Wood
if I approached her gently – as I cood –
for Julia's not a babe in any Wood;

yes, I believe that Julia truly Wood,
she's not fictitious like Red Riding Hood.
Julia Wood like to! I'm sure Julia Wood!

To Margo

In life's rough-and-tumble
you're the crumble on my apple crumble
and the fairy on my Christmas tree!
In life's death-and-duty
you've the beauty of the Beast's own Beauty –
I feel humble as a bumble-bee!

In life's darkening duel
I'm the lighter, you're the lighter fuel –
and the tide that sways my inland sea!
In life's meet-and-muster
you've the lustre of a diamond cluster –
a blockbuster – just a duster, me!

A Possible Line of William Empson

A tie, in dining cars, commands respect

An Exeter Riddle

Sitters on the mead-bench, quaffing among questions,
I saw a thing – tell me its totality.
A boy sped by, his feet did not grind gravel,
high was his head, incautious in the company
of the might of mountains and a rock-rent liquid.
His hands moved little, his legs seemed listless,
yet he woke the wind and exacerbated echoes,
wending not to war in a charging chariot,
unhelped by horses, whirling like the wind.
Test-tube technology covered him completely.

Seamus Heaney

He's very popular among his mates.
I think I'm Auden. He thinks he's Yeats.

Haiku: The Wit and Wisdom of Cyril Connolly

Connolly called the
British 'sheep with a nasty
side'. How very true!

A Titled Lady

At once a picture comes into my mind of a stately
beauty, topless perhaps, being manoeuvred into a ballroom
by a burly footman. He walks slowly backwards, firmly
grasping one of her excited nipples in each white-gloved hand.

In the Land of Vowel-Reversed Rhyming

Now strippers everywhere flaunt their white loins
in King's Arms, Dukes and Bulls and the White Lions –
full in the face, to Puritans, vitriol
but welcome to the tillers of the soil
(Scot granite to the Western clay, lias),
who love to watch them wriggle on the dais.
From mountain crofts and flat alluvial plains,
the Dais and Hodges, Micks and Joes and Ians,
combine with Rams, Aquarians and Leos
to worship birds and bushes, tits and toes.

Not Wavell But Browning

Nobody read him, the poor sod,
He was always moaning:
I am much more way out than you think
And not Wavell but Browning.

Poor chap, he always loved Larkin
And now he's dead,
The critics were too cold for him, his art gave way
They said.

Oh, no no no, they were too cold always
(He still never stopped moaning)
I was obscene and avant-garde and obscure
And not Wavell but Browning.

NOTE   Wavell was the British general of the Second World War who edited
a conservative anthology of English verse called *Other Men's Flowers*. To the
Victorians, Browning was the last word in newness and incomprehensibility.

North American Haiku

Hail, tribes of Outer
Alcoholia – the Rednose
and Goutfoot Indians!

Alcohol

Oh, so slowly the brain starts to go
as the cells are burned out, row by row,
and they're never replaced –
so we're certainly faced
with oblivion – the last thing we know!

Tourist Traffic

If you're in the market for fucks or
a girl or a boy who just sucks or
desire an Egyptian
of any description –
get going on a slow boat to Luxor.

Double Haiku: Sexism

All the tall thin gay
solicitors tell their boy
friends how women are,

without exception,
about three feet tall at most,
with big smelly cunts.

Haiku: Mrs X

An old police dog
sniffs my knickers. I charge him
£8,000. Wow!

Haiku: Foreplay

Undressing, she laugh-
ingly hung her panties on
his hard hatrack cock.

Found Haiku: Waterloo Station Gents

I want to whip the
bare bottom of a pretty
girl tied up for it.

Variation on Two Lines of W. B. Yeats

Love is staying for a bit
in the place of piss and shit.

Drinking Song

Elated by the Great Depressant,
I was feeling fine.
Bottle, glass and lip – incessant
was the flow of wine!

Why on earth should people stop?
Drink it down to the last drop!

Ah, but wines have lees and dregs too,
they can turn the brain,
easily knock you off your legs too,
drive you quite insane,
there's an end to all the jokes
in the heart attacks and strokes!

T. S. Eliot and Ezra Pound

Eliot loved the music halls
(and he probably loved pantos).
Pound took the rubbish out of *The Waste Land*
and put it all into the *Cantos*.

Not Peace But A Sword

Mosque or temple, church or steeple,
religions are keenest
on killing people!

Ruperta Bear's Feminist Poem

We live in a society that's phallocratic
but we're beginning to make literature cunnicentric.
Already many women can only read books by women –
if they accidentally read something written by a MAN
at once a horrible feeling comes over them,
the words grip them like the hands of a rapist,
with a scream they throw the book from them!

A Betjeman Variation
(Tune: 'Red Sails in the Sunset')

As hot as a hornet,
As warm as a wasp,
They're dying like flies in
The old Cottage Hosp!

Celtic

The Irish are great talkers,
persuasive and disarming.
You can say lots and lots
against the Scots –
but at least they're never charming!

All Marriages Are Mixed

Did the Greeks have a word for it
(marital boredom)?
As every day they gazed at the same old face
from Samothrace?

The Sadness of Cricket

(many facts from *The Golden Age of Cricket 1890–1914* by
David Frith)

The happy summer game, where fun
lies like a playful cat in golden sun –
true innocence in every ball and every run –

where all is for the best, they say,
nostalgia only when it goes away –
romantic memories that haunt the close of play –

is like that poem, 'Dover Beach',
like Arnold's lovely world it's out of reach,
and there are other lessons it might also teach.

How golden lads of Housman's sort
lose all that beauty and can end up caught –
by portliness – and far too fond of gin and port.

And how the agile cover point
slows with arthritis in each stiffened joint –
his briskest fielding now would only disappoint.

Those godlike carefree flashing blades
don't flash for ever in that field of shades
and time can trump a Trumper like an ace of spades.

All right for private incomes, turn
to them they could, money they had to burn,
the amateurs, the Gentlemen! But Players earn

their living in a young man's game –
when they retire it's never quite the same.
If they despaired, would they be very much to blame?

Coaches and pros at public schools,
they taught the rudiments to flannelled fools;
like swimmers striking out in private swimming pools,

the young were trained in all the strokes.
But did *they* feel like victims of a hoax?
Famous fast bowlers, run to fat, now schoolboy jokes?

We'd one at Wellington, that A. E. Relf,
who'd bowled for England – long since on the shelf –
in 1937 stalled and shot himself.

Remembered bowling in the nets,
a little irritable (I thought – but one forgets),
doling out stumps to junior games, like doubtful debts,

from the Pavilion's mean back door.
He had this job, I wouldn't think him poor,
but losing it might put him firmly on the floor.

Professionals lose jobs? They could.
Respectful, yes, you had to be – and 'good'.
Some amateurs cut loose, but it was understood

that there was really no appeal
(although it seems to me a dodgy deal)
when Players misbehaved; witness the case of Peel,

a Yorkshire bowler, too content
to stay in the beer tent, his favourite tent.
A Test Match bowler too, but did Lord Hawke relent?

Peed on the pitch! A County game
was scene of his unheard-of drunken shame.
Hawke threw him out; and Peel's a long-forgotten name.

Pro with a County? Umpire? Then
that was 'retirement' for such humble men.
Cricket Schools? Sports goods? These were rare in 1910.

Though Gunn made bats. The 'Autograph'
by Gunn & Moore, his sporting epitaph.
Used once by me. My batting, though, would make you laugh.

Strength, talent gone – then what to do?
Great Albert Trott, like Relf, was gunned down too
by his own hand in Willesden – very sad but true.

'His powers waned in 1904'
the record says – and just £4, no more,
was found, his wardrobe left to landlady. The score

of that fine bowler/batsman: small.
'He liked a pint'; but dropsy took it all.
In 1914 – thousands more about to fall –

Harry Graham and Johnny Briggs
died in asylums – and among the prigs
who wouldn't fancy Burns (corn rigs and barley rigs)

you might count batsman A. E. Knight,
'mental' perhaps, at least not over-bright,
who prayed while batting – an extraordinary sight!

And Arthur Shrewsbury, tipped by Grace
as runner-up in the Great Batsman Race –
he was a suicide. He couldn't stand the pace;

thousands of runs that he amassed
made Grace a generous enthusiast
but didn't help. And Aubrey Faulkner, too, was gassed

in London, 1930, by
his own sad hand. It makes you want to cry –
but all they wanted was some peace, simply to die.

And Arthur Woodcock also went,
in 1910, by his own poison sent
to that far bourne. Each cricket season was lent

to Leicestershire. He coached the lads
at an American College; and their Dads
remembered him as fast as Kortright. Oiks and cads

such may have been. At 44
he thought it time to leave and shut the door . . .
The Gentlemen had deaths as well, but in the War.

Poor Stoddart was another case,
who shared great opening partnerships with Grace –
but shot himself at 52. Life's hard to face!

The blazer and the ribboned coat?
The most pathetic soul for Charon's boat
was Percy Frederick Hardy – he just cut his throat

at King's Cross Station; old and mean,
the Fates attacked him, March 1916.
Ten years for Somerset, a useful pro, he'd been

scared of the Front, the shells, the mud.
A public lavatory received his blood.
The County of London Yeomanry found him a dud.

The Captains toss. It's Head or Tails;
but Time and Death at last remove the bails,
though you weep buckets of the Bard's prophetic pails.

You can work gents into the mix.
George Lohmann died (T.B.) at 36,
and Alfred Lyttelton was himself hit for six –

an abscess from a cricket ball,
a Cabinet Minister when toffs walked tall.
A famous Foster was most interesting of all.

A tart was murdered, and police
knew that he knew her. Questions didn't cease,
frequent as cigarette burns on a mantelpiece.

He took her home (200 fags,
a bottle of Scotch whisky bought – old bags
like this) but she was young and not the kind that nags.

At 20 Nora Upchurch had
gone loose in London – also to the bad.
Strangled in Shaftesbury Avenue (that's also trad).

An empty house. A man called Field
confessed to Press, and all was then 'revealed'
that for two years had been quite well concealed.

'Not guilty' at Old Bailey (he
retracted all he'd said), in '33
he walked away, he was released, completely free.

But later tried the same trick twice.
This time the jury turned out not so nice.
You win some, lose some, it's the shaking of the dice.

Nobody gets away with much.
Even late cuts, the Ranjitsinhji touch,
leg glances, don't impress the Fates and gods and such.

A Gorgon married C. B. Fry.
Call no man lucky till he's come to die;
So said the Greeks, and they had ancient reasons why.

NOTES

1   *Victor Trumper* (1877–1915) One of the greatest Australian batsmen. Like
Grace and Hobbs, he could make high scores on very difficult wickets. He
died at the age of 35.

2   *Bobby Peel* Yorkshire bowler (Yorkshire won the County Championship nine
times between 1893 and 1912). He took 102 Test wickets against Australia; once
winning a Test by ten runs (taking 8 for 67) but had to be sobered up in a cold
shower beforehand by his Captain.

3   *William Gunn* A great Nottinghamshire and England batsman (George Gunn
was his only slightly less famous brother). In 1896 he went on strike, refusing
to play in a Test team unless he was paid £20, instead of the usual £10. He
died a wealthy man – because of his partnership in Gunn & Moore.

4   *Albert Trott* An Australian bowler with several styles, and a tremendous hitter.
He took 8 for 43 in his first Test against England. When the selectors ignored
him, he played as a pro for Middlesex (4 wickets in 4 balls and later a hat-trick
against Somerset, in his benefit match in 1907). In 1899 and 1900 made over
1,000 runs, took 200 wickets in each season. An umpire in 1910.

5   *Albert Knight* Went to Australia with P. F. Warner's team of 1903–04. He is slandered in the poem, since he was apparently 'thoughtful and well-read'. Nevertheless the Lancashire fast bowler Walter Brearley is supposed to have reported him to the M.C.C. for praying during an innings.

6   *Arthur Shrewsbury* The greatest professional batsman of the 1880s and 1890s. His 164 on a dangerous pitch in the Lord's Test of 1886, against the bowling of Spofforth, is reckoned one of the finest innings ever played. He was an opening batsman of extraordinary patience. He captained England in seven Tests in Australia. Committed suicide in 1903, aged 47.

7   *Aubrey Faulkner* A South African Test cricketer, who also played for the Gentlemen. Very successful in the 1909–10 series against England. A D.S.O. in the War.

8   *Arthur Woodcock* Described as 'a magnificent specimen of Midlands manhood'. Kortright was the fastest bowler of his day, and at his best Woodcock was thought to be as fast.

9   *A. E. Stoddart* Captain of England at cricket and rugby. While leading England in the 1894–95 tour, he made 173 at Melbourne – highest score by an England captain in Australia until 1975. In his last match for Middlesex in 1900 he scored 221. His opening partnerships with W. G. Grace were legendary. He shot himself in 1915, soon after his 52nd birthday.

10   *Percy Frederick Hardy* He was a Dorset-born left-hander, but played for Somerset. Top score: 91 against Kent at Taunton in 1910.

11   *George Lohmann* One of the 'strikers' of 1896, and a principal professional bowler for Surrey. Took 100 wickets, for example, in 1892 – when Surrey were Champions for the third year running.

12   *Alfred Lyttleton* Brother-in-law of Arthur Balfour, Prime Minister. Wicket-keeper batsman for Eton, Cambridge, Middlesex, Worcestershire, the Gentlemen and England. In 1884, in a Test at the Oval, he removed his wicket-keeper's pads and took 4 for 19 with underarm lobs. In 1913, when he was 56, a blow from the ball caused an internal abscess – from which he died.

13   *The Fosters* This was F.R. Foster, who led Warwickshire to the Championship in 1911, at the age of 22, making a century in both Yorkshire matches and 200 against Surrey. He took 32 wickets that winter, in a very successful tour of Australia. But the strain showed in 1912, and he rested for a year. Nevertheless he made 305 not out against Worcestershire in 1914 (still the County record). A motorcycle accident during the War put an end to his cricketing career. He was a left arm fast bowler and a right-handed batsman. He had no connection with the seven Foster brothers who played for Worcestershire, of whom the most famous, R.E. ('Tip') Foster, captained England and died young, at 36, of diabetes. For details of the Field case, see *A Reasonable Doubt* by Julian Symons.

14   *K. S. Ranjitsinhji* The famous Indian Prince who played for Cambridge, Sussex and England. A great stylist, he was the first man to score 3,000 runs in a season.

15   *C. B. Fry* The blue-eyed boy. Scholar, athlete, footballer (Association and Rugby Union), journalist, Naval officer, schoolmaster. Played for Sussex and England. Six successive First Class centuries in 1901 (still a record). Married Beatrice Sumner, a very tough lady who (after his death) took over command of a training ship for Royal Naval cadets, forbidding all masturbation, dumb insolence and answering back.

Tribes

('*Here's tae us – wha's like us?*')

Are tribes a good thing?
Or are they bad, and ugly –
as smugly they hug themselves
over a victory, football or cricket
or almost anything?

Irish, Welsh or Scots –
should they pride themselves so
on Kelso? do they smell so
terrifically sweet? what about their feet?
English, Irish, Welsh or Scots?

You could pride yourself
on looking like Cardinal Newman,
on being a woman or human
or deft or left-handed, or 'gentry' or 'landed'.
You *could* pride yourself.

But it's all a bit fake,
a bit bogus and silly –
a big willie, being a hillbilly,
most pride is foolish, stubborn and mulish
but in the end a bit fake!

Lovers In Pairs

Hearing the other one breathe
is a function of all paired sleepers
   and it's coupled with the wish
   such breathing should not stop.

Young lovers lay ears to hearts
and say how it would be ghastly
   if the beating faded down
   to silence – just gone away.

They think the end of the one
would be love's end, for no other
   ever would be the same.
   Of course, they're right – and wrong,

for many will come to the beds
and twenty is different from thirty,
   as sentiment's middle age
   moves slowly and coolly on.

When old ones lie side by side
what's real at last has a look-in.
   The breathing *could*, surely, stop –
   and with it the warmth of love.

It's the penultimate bed
before the one with the gravestone.
   This is what each one thinks –
   a thought sad, loving and warm.

Incoming Calls

They come in so happily, the incoming calls!
Stepping gaily into a room –
a room, it could be, of depression or mourning,
of someone whose sister has just died of cancer,
whose cat has been run over,
whose boyfriend or girlfriend has gone for ever . . .

The jollity of the far voices halts on the doormat,
as it were. The old friend feeling good
and wanting a long amusing chat
feels out of place, a tactless intruder.
He or she. Shut the door and stumble away –
            ring off –

that's all they can do.

Putney OAPs in 1985

They dribble down the High Street/ in dribs and drabs,
   on sticks,
the wrinkle-faced old women,/ the men with 'past it' pricks,
slow among the mums who/ wrestle with push-chair kids,
they stop for 'Hello, stranger!s'/ or 'Well, I never did!s',
clots in the pavement's bloodstream/ that bike-boys put at risk,
they wince at teenage swearing,/ tut-tutting or tsk- tsk!
When Thatcher was a nothing/ and keen on boys or horses,
they underwent the bombing,/ and the danger of the Forces.
MPs who live for money/ and the well-being of the City
don't reckon much these old ones,/ they're a bore, a drag,
   a pity –
not beautiful, attractive,/ fashionable or bright,
why can't they get a move on/ into that long goodnight?

They don't appear on chat shows,/ not many ask their views,
they're has-beens of the media,/ they never will be news.

So close down the old people's/ hospitals and homes
(the Welfare State, quite clearly,/ isn't loved by well-fed
   gnomes),
forget the War they fought in,/ way out beyond the brink –
because it *doesn't matter*/ what such old seniles think!

All Souls

This is the room where the great poet breathed his last.
His breathtaking originality is now like mist on the air.
Here is the desk where he worked, and in the corner
is the old wind-up gramophone that helped him when he typed.

There are photos of friends, and letters: *Cher collègue*!
In glass-fronted bookcases are his books, including his
Collected Poems translated into Icelandic.

In the master-bedroom there are photographs of his wife.
She has less of an aura, but nonetheless she is there.
He is the star, the children are photo-appendages, like the small
groups, quite informal, of him with the great Other Writers.
He didn't have much taste in pictures, the landscapes are dullish.
To show honesty, perhaps to shock, is a detailed line-drawing
of the small obstinate penis that caused him so much trouble.
Some love-letters survive, with the work-sheets of verse.
There are even, like sleeping beauties, curled locks of their hair.

The There Then meets the Here Now in piped appropriate
music, its fixed harmonies run like lost dogs through the rooms.
His walking stick too lies doglike in a glass case.
It will never walk again, 'it has finished with walking',
as his pupil expressed it in the famous memorial poem.

The Daytime Mugging in the High Street

Who would want to attack that poor little thing
walking up Putney High Street at 9.30 in the morning,
without a thought in her head except to get to Putney
    BR Station
and then to Clapham Junction, to a sale at Arding & Hobbs,
with a view to buying a quilt, or was it a fan-heater?
Well, somebody did! Went for her purse in her basket,
pushed her into the road. Severe bruising, three lower vertebrae
    cracked.
A young chap, he missed the purse, made off into Fulham.

I reckon he was a loony; or an addict, crazy on a Monday
    morning,
needing a fix after the weekend. Who knows? She didn't even
    see him.
Luckily for her, there wasn't any traffic. Thrown into a
    main road,
she could have been killed. All the conventional judgments
say what a terrible thing (true) and what a terrible man!
But I say, too, she *might* still be better off than a tormented
    young junkie.

The Garrotting

('It's an Old Spanish Custom')

In an Exhibition devoted to the Art of Barcelona
there is this picture of a public execution –
I marvel at the date – 1894!
But no, it's in modern dress, a crowd in a big square,
the seated victim, the hypocrites crowding round,
telling him Jesus loves him as the iron collar tightens,
the executioner turns the screw that's boring in

below the skull, to kill the spinal cord.
Are the men in pointed hats the Inquisition?
This is Old Spanish Cruelty. The suffering
benefits sadists only, a threat, something to show
that *status quo* has meaning in the world.

I think of Larkin's hard throat cancer death,
better than being garrotted – but not much.

NOTE   The last public execution in Britain took place in 1866.

The Poets' Revolt

In Poetry Review *(Volume 75, Number 4) there is a League Table
of the living British and Irish poets, divided into four Divisions,
as in the Football League. This list begins with all the H's –
Heaney, Hughes, Hill, Harrison (in that order). This is the work
of John Sheeran, of Oxford University. Altogether, 92 poets are
'placed'.*

Heaney is the only one
who'll be pleased with what he's done –
you can't say the same for Hughes,
Laureates hate being Number 2s.
You don't need a Holmes or Freud
to guess they'll *all* be quite annoyed
to see that they've been ranked below
frauds and pseuds like So-and-So.
Kit Wright numbered 89 –
put down so far he's in a mine!
One First Division woman (20) –
one woman only, and that's plenty –
that seems to be the general gist
of this dreaded donlike list.
And Wendy Cope at 91!

Surely it would be quite fun
(and poets, surely, should be able)

to make a *Critical* League Table
where all the dons who love to spout
and splash like whales and swim about
had numbers stuck upon their backs.
All open to harpoon attacks.
Guess who'd be bottom! Just guess who!
Sheeran! Like Patten (92)!

'Sex in the Soapsuds'

(*Found poem,* Wandsworth & Putney Guardian, *30 January 1986*)

Romping Romeos indulge in steamy launderette love-ins
while their dirty linen is washing.
As their clothes tumble in the dryer
they tumble sexily in the soapsuds.
And their lust is getting launderette owners in a lather.
This is just one of the vices soiling
the whiter-than-white image of our launderettes.
Laundry staff allege that customers
have sex in front of washing machines
sniff glue and smoke pot
beat up staff
intimidate managers
spit on old ladies' clean undies . . .

Mavie Nolan, who works at the Coin-op, Bedford Hill,
says she can hardly believe
how people abuse her launderette.
'I come in and a couple are having sex.'

Sally

'Are you interested in knowing *when and whom you will marry?
What the year will bring you? If you will gain in a lawsuit? . . . What
are you best adapted for? If you have enemies and who? If you can trust
your friends? Why your love acts strange? What lies in the future and
what fate awaits you?*'

– New York street handout

Anglo-Saxon Sally operates between Third and Lexington –
she makes large claims:
'Forecasts – Future – Past – Present
with Palm, Tarot Cards, Crystal Ball, Readings'.
Are her clients all dames?

Or does the SPECIAL WITH THIS AD Regular Card Reading
$5.00 OFF
offered to the street-passers
pull in young, confused, gullible, male New Yorkers,
chauvinist at the pig-trough?

Tune in to these thoughts: 'Why don't that Marylene let me
touch up her ass?'
'Why she act so strange, man?'
It doesn't seem likely, probable – or possible even.
No, a different class,

the unsure more-than-mature woman is here targeted.
'That Mrs Feinblatt,
she look at me in a funny way!'
'Ed don't love me any more. He think I'm done for, past it!'
'Mr Fink's a dirty rat.'

Or just a bit younger? When Romance can be mentioned,
Love that will last.
'Will Wilbur ever kiss me?'
Sally knows these thoughts like the colour of the dollars,
forecasting the Past.

June 1985

A Wee Laberlethin For the Lads Wi' the Lallans

(See *The Concise Scots Dictionary 1985*)

Och, lackanee! alas! an' wae!
The Muse o' birse-cups an' the brae,
yon lammie-meh ye cuddle tae,
   she's aiblins left ye
an' o' the sense tae sing or say
   she's sure bereft ye!

D'ye no mind John Logie Baird,
wha rules the soun' waves lek a laird,
wha blins the sicht till nane are spared,
   an' fettles baith –
gars mak a lame, a mant, a *merde*
   wi' laidron laith?

Ye lawbour on your lawboards still,
but Telly taps Parnassus Hill,
ye hae the bensell an the will
   but still ye're waitin'
the Muse – an' she'll be missin' till
   ye write i' Laitin!

Lacklustre labsters! Lampeekoo
is a' ye're fit for here an' noo,
lawins an' lounrie when ye're fou,
   lampin' alang
wi' sic lamgabblich – as a coo
   might mak a sang!

Ye'll not owercome the pow'r o' Ringo,
or a' the glamourie o' Bingo,
or Sex, flumgummery flamingo –
   high-kiltit verse
will aye be in their lugs laich lingo
   an' Fame's reverse!

Ye laik, ye laig, ye lauch, ye lagger,
ye claut the laggin till ye stagger –

lak lacrissye they laib Mick Jagger,
  your lays stir anger,
lang lugs, ye slay lek dirk or dagger
  wi' fearfu' langour!

Knapdarlocks, in your kneggum strang,
fa' silent, ye hae sung owerlang
the Scots your kickmaleeries wrang!
  Leave th' kilfuddoch!
Ye've nae mair apitude for sang
  than th' puir puddock!

GLOSSARY

laberlethin a rigmarole, rambling discourse (la 19th–20thC)
lackanee alas (la 19thC)
birse-cup final cup of tea with whisky instead of milk (e20thC)
lammie-meh pet name for a lamb (e20thC)
fettle go for (a person) (la 19thC)
lame a critical injury (15–e16thC)
mant a stutter, a stammer (19thC)
laidron rascal, loafer (16thC)
laith evil (la 14th–15thC)
lawbour = labour
lawboard (*Labrod*) lapboard, a board laid across the knees for working on (19th–e20thC)
bensell force, violence (la 17th–e20thC)
lampeekoo a variation of hide-and-seek
lawins a session of drinking, esp. in a tavern (16th–17thC)
lounrie sexual wickedness, fornication (la 16th–e18thC)
lamp stride along (17thC)
lamgabblich a long rambling discourse, a rigmarole (20thC)
glamourie = glamour (18thC–e20thC)
flumgummery any foolish or frivolous thing
high-kiltit having the skirts well tucked up, immodest, indecent (la 18th–e20thC)
laich low (la 14thC)
laik amuse oneself (15th–16thC)
laig chatter (la 19thC)
lauch laugh (la 14thC)
lagger sink in mud or soft ground (18thC)
claut the laggin drain a container of drink (la 18th–19thC)
lacrissye liquorice (la 15th–16thC)
laib lick up, lap, gobble (18thC)
lang lugs a donkey (a person with long ears) (18thC)
langour boredom (la 15thC)
knapdarlock hardened dirt or dung hanging from the tail of an animal, a dirty, cheeky
  person (1., la 19thC, 2. 20thC)
kneggum disagreeable taste or flavour (la 18thC)
kickmaleerie a flimsy trifling thing (19thC)
kilfuddoch a meeting and discussion (19thC)
puddock a toad (or frog) (la 16thC)

Kingsley Has a Go at a Latin Poem

Stabat mulier beata,
omnibus conspicua, mammeata,
invidia multis iam conflata!

Praeclara tamen stat papilla,
odor fragrans in axilla,
meretrix, nomine Camilla!

Centuriones sunt amentes,
Venus flagellat omnes gentes,
cupidines non sunt absentes.

Magnitudo erectionum
optimum eis certe bonum,
plaudunt, magnum faciunt sonum.

Miraculum labia maiora
sed autem, quae sunt meliora,
dulcissima labia minora!

Amantium precationes
et ejaculationes
longae sicut orationes!

Languescunt, partem femineam
illae Camillae pensant ream.
Laudunt omnes illam deam!

Translation   A happy woman was standing, in the sight of all, big-breasted,
the envy of many straightway excited! Very beautiful, in the same way,
stands out the nipple, there is a fragrant odour in the armpit – she is a
harlot, by name Camilla! The centurions are out of their minds, Venus lashes
all the nations, desires are not absent. The size of their erections is to them,
for certain, of the highest good, they applaud, they make a great noise. A
wonder to see her labia majora – but moreover, what are even better, her
very sweet labia minora! The prayers of her lovers, and their ejaculations,
are as long as public speeches! They faint with languor, they consider the
womanly part of that Camilla to be the cause. All praise that goddess!

NOTE   The Rev. Charles Kingsley, best known as the author of *The Water*

Babies, Westward Ho! and a handful of poems, was remarkable for his belief that life in Heaven consisted of never-ending sexual intercourse – a belief not common in his lifetime (1819–1875). His model here is the rhymed poem in Latin written by monks in the Middle Ages, usually a hymn.

The Last Days of Old Poets

Many old poets are dead, that were thought of by me once
    as rivals,
    enemies even, deadbeats, and arrogant terrible pseuds.
Edith Sitwell, e.g. (though of course she's an older example).
    Bandersnatches abound; on the wartime trek round the pubs
Tambimuttu was there, as they all played 'Follow My Leader',
    the Fitzroy, the Wheatsheaf, and then the *Caves de France* and
    the French,
that was the evening round – but the one thing lacking
    was talent.
    Or so I used to think. Though Maclaren-Ross was good,
David Archer had charm, like a left-wing Bertie Wooster.
    You can't blame them – a boring war, and not much to do
    but drink . . .
But now as the dogs catch up, the travelling Hounds of Heaven.
    and pull us down one by one, the stag, the rat, the mouse,
I feel more mellow to them – for the death that we have in
    common –
    companions of my youth, that people hated and loved,
tattered and torn and old, that once amazed with their
    brightness,
    the other side of that war – the deepest, darkest ditch
between what was young and this Now, as I begin to feel tender
    to those who survived (or not). But still are a part of me.

Byron's Problem

When they come up to you, as you're sitting quietly,
and lay their fat boobs on your knees,
and look into your eyes with their own big eyes
and wistfully caress your cheek
and so, without speaking, say 'Please!'
it's a clear invitation to come out and play
and you can't just tell them to go away!

When the wine's round and they press up against you gently,
it's much like a musicless waltz
as they talk about books (and they all write books) –
that's *foreplay*, nothing else, my son,
true sex; it's the talking that's false!
But you can't make a snarky and sharpish riposte,
with words like 'Forget it!', 'Get lost!'

When they stroke your hair too, and finger your coat slyly,
or lay a neat hand on your shirt,
they all cast you as Faust (and they all know Faust),
each one's a Gretchen, maiden, pure;
but they all want your hand up their skirt.
So men of great talent must pay this high price,
and no one will think that you're terribly nice!

Written in honour of Byron's Bicentenary (he was born in 1788).
He once claimed that he was 'raped' by the highborn
intellectual young ladies after he became famous.

Ecossaise

'*The Scottish melodic idiom seems to be absent from all the tunes to which the name is given. Beethoven, Chopin and Schubert have left écossaises for piano, and there is nothing Scottish about any of them.*' – Percy Scholes, The Oxford Companion To Music

Like Robert Louis Stevenson living in Samoa,
like George MacBeth living in Sheffield,
like Ian Brady living in Greater Manchester,

I am a Scotsman living in exile; my father
was the first of the family to fly south –
my grandfather stayed, a professor in Edinburgh.

My mother was of mixed blood, with some from Buchanans
who went to New Zealand, then came back again.
She was at least half English, she didn't know Lallans.

We lived in London. We went, as you might say, native.
We were eating long-pig and cooking the breadfruit,
beachcombers, cast off from the as-it-were-civilized whalers.

This meant that as kids or wee bairns or children
she walked us often across Hyde Park to Harrods
with her dogs which were always Scottish terriers – bewildered

by any intercultural shock we were not, a change of houses
would have meant more; we accepted it all, as the
Kanakas (bullied by the missionaries) gave up a kilt for trousers.

After all, we were born there. Cricket seemed natural.
A tartan was just a pattern (though we did choose Buchanan).
We gave no thought to Scotland – our thinking wasn't lateral.

There were memories of Burns and acquaintance with whisky
but our politics and newspapers and governments
had only one word, stiff-lipped, riding to hounds: England.

Oh, others have done it. I think you might cite Byron,
he was a Gordon. My dad, with his half-caste wife,
went after Success, the foreign and feminine Siren.

Snow White

She's a widow-maker
and a credit-taker,
everything good's due to *her* –
it's not accident,
she's Heaven-sent,
she can only sit and purr

as the cream grows richer
and the culture kitscher –
and there's no dissenting voice
as the topcats scoff it
and the god called Profit
is the South East English Choice

and the Press grows hottish
as the traitor Scottish
beg to differ a bit;
while the BBC too
she must certainly see to
with her Instant Pressure Kit!

There is homeless weeping
but her Good Housekeeping
will make us happy and strong
and the Future fissile
through each new missile –
you don't get those for a song.

The Falklands Factor
or a dodgy reactor,
she takes them all in her stride,
nothing loth, nothing lother –

the Contras, Piet Botha!
She's not just there for the ride.

Queen of every chat show,
the Crystal Cat Show
never ever produced such a cat,
worshipped by Wogan,
her personal slogan:
I'm right, never wrong! And that's that!

Girl Squash

In 1936 at the age of about fifteen
Alan Ross played squash with a girl
who worked at Government House –
she had some Indian, or perhaps Chinese, blood.
Her skin, he says, was 'pure ivory'.
Afterwards, in her flat in Bhawanipore Road,
they would take it in turns to shower.
'Look at me if you like' she once said to him,
letting her towel fall open.
No sex, but she was kindly (less than ten years older).

This was Calcutta.
In about 1948, when I was thirty-two,
I played squash with a girl called Nicole Onoff –
she must have been about the same age as Ross's girl.

She was partly Russian, partly (I think) French.
She was friendly, sturdy, very athletic,
played hockey for England and was also,
I believe, an Olympic diving champion.
She played to keep fit; I could just beat her,
but only if I ran like a demon.
Drop shots and lobs were no part of our armoury.
No sex, naturally. I guarded the shower
while she was using it – to forestall intruders.

Then we bicycled away, separately.
From the Oatlands Park Hotel –
because this was in Weybridge.

Freud

I first met Lucian when I was a friend of Spender's
at Stephen's flat (I've always been a friend of Spender's)
in 1938 or 1939 – I would be twenty-three and he would be
    seventeen.
In 1939 he would be seventeen.
This wasn't much of a meeting; but we were in the same room,
it has to count as a meeting, if you're in the same room
and introduced, as we were. Ah, but the next time!

There was something very different about the next time!
I remember it like a dream, I was walking by Green Park –
down Piccadilly, by the summer-green Green Park,
on my way to catch a bus home at Hyde Park Corner,
and all the way from Green Park station to Hyde Park Corner
he followed me, saying *Gavin Ewart is a terrible person*
and attacking my character, saying what a terrible person
I was. I cowered. I wasn't used to such attacks,
I'd done nothing whatever to deserve such attacks,
I was innocent and unsophisticated. What could I answer?
I now realize I should have stopped walking, and made
    an answer.
Was he drunk, or on drugs – or was it a fugue?
Is that sort of thing what the shrinks call a fugue?

At about that time Stephen showed me a photo of Lucian at the
    age of nine,
like a small beaky bird, at the age of nine –
saying how sweet he looked. That was the last time I saw him;
in Piccadilly was the last time I saw him.

But I heard about him, later that year, from Ian Lubbock
when he had married Lys. My girlfriend. Next, Mrs Lubbock.

In 1939, I would guess. He came home one day, he told me,
and found *Lys in bed with Freud* – that's what he told me.
He didn't seem worried; it was like a piece of gossip.
And the next time I heard about him it was genuine gossip:
Lucian was very clever at the time of his call up!
When they interviewed him at his call up,
he told them he always had a funny feeling
in a room full of men – a very funny feeling.
And he said he couldn't leave his little cat,
he didn't think he could go into the army and leave his little cat.

This may have been malicious, but it was quite entertaining.

And if anybody thinks these jottings are entertaining
they're quite welcome to use them. In a *Lives Of The Great*
Portrait Painters
for example. I think he deserves to have his life in a *Lives Of The*
Great Portrait Painters.

Sailing to Byzantium

(A 61st Anniversary Version)

That's no place for oldies, where the kids
are having it off all over, and treeborne birds
(and they snuff it, each and every) sing!
The salmon fool about in the rivers, macks in the sea,
swimmers, runners, flyers through all the summer
are hyping all that's born and kicks the bucket.
And in that woozy music nobody pays heed
to the books of the highbrows and the string
quartets!

An old guy is, sure, a no-account thing,
some threads on a broomstick, if he don't
make with the soul and bust the ozone

in proportion as he's looking kinda crumby.
And they don't care for getting the joint jumping,
all they want is to admire their own star quality.
So for these reasons I booked a steerage passage
and now I'm in God's Own City – Byzantium.

You wise guys standing in God's Holy Fire
like in those mosaic things on walls,
unwind for a moment, you old honey-buzzards,
and give me a lead – I wanna make some music!
Eat my heart out, by golly! It's got the hots
for something, it's lost its identity, it's stuck with
an animal that's gonna croak! So just take me
into the make-believe they call Eternity!

Once I've handed in my dinner pail
I'll never wanna be a living man or beast,
but more like stuff some Greeks made out of gold –
gold and enamel, say, by bashing it with hammers
to keep some dopey Emperor from hitting the hay.
Or the clockwork birds they put on golden branches
to sing to the high-class guys and dolls of Byzantium
of what's been and gone, what's new, or in the stars yet!

W. B. Yeats, 1927. Gavin Ewart, 1988.

A Patient of Dr Rycroft's

Today I am feeling comatic.
After a long night with Kit.
But all love is infantilistic
and even reactionary men
have no sense of structure –
even the most sensitive are incapable
of lasting personal relationships.

I regard all sex as masturbatory,
there's no point in kissing or 'foreplay'.

I have my language, you have yours.
A lowerarchy is a hierarchy viewed from above.
You laughed when you asked me
'Were you annoyed?'
and I answered 'Annoyed? I was paranoid!'

Suffixes, prefixes? Who fixes them? I fix them.
There's iron in irony, although you smile.
Socrates? How does he come into it?
I don't understand metaphors,
semaphores and meaningless signals.
'Getting something off my chest'
means a bra or a boyfriend.
Things are things, and not other things.

You're surprised I call them 'lovers' –
I have so many of them.
Most, you say, would mistrust, distrust
such casual encounters. I have no fear,
once a teenage pillion rider on a wall of death.
Just as I have no social shyness.

At ten I decided to be Shakespeare, and a ventriloquist.
At seventeen I wrote a poem identical with one of Verlaine's
and a melody identical with one by Rachmaninov.
I could have been a great ballerina.
I have telepathic powers.
Freud, you say – 'sexual overestimation of the ego'.

But I have my effigies, and my own theory.
'Physically real internal figures'.
I worked it out myself,
with the help of two books,
one by Reik and one by Reich.
I want to be a child analyst.

Distelligent, sensationful, miswanted –
you smile at my vocabulary – but I still love cats.
If there are 'love-objects'

in this world, they are cats.
They are overstanding.
All mothers are sadistic.

I am beautiful and an actress.
I also believe I can find a way to be immortal.

See the case history 'Miss Y: The Analysis of a Paranoid Personality'
contained in *Psychoanalysis and Beyond* by Charles Rycroft. 'Reactionary' =
sensitive, in her vocabulary. People who 'have no sense of structure' do not
want lasting relationships.

Sonnet: The Scene at 29 Ratcliffe Highway in 1811

Inside the shop, the body of James Gowen (14), apprentice –
his head battered to pulp, brains on the ceiling, blood
    everywhere –
by the door, Mrs Marr (24). The same.
Behind the counter, the body of Timothy Marr (24). Ditto.
In the basement the baby (3 months), face battered, throat cut
    through.
'Most inhumanly and barbarously murdered,' said the Home
    Secretary.

'A sickly sweet smell of blood and brains,' say the crime writers.
General panic. Fear and hate for Portuguese and Irish.

Next, all four corpses laid out on beds. But no
restrictions on sightseers. Neighbours. Fine ladies. The stench of
    Wapping,
the press and mill of stinking living bodies,
'the first sickly-sweet intimations of decay',
the inquest four days later. Horror would overpower –
but what would shake *us* most would be the smell.

See *The Maul and the Pear Tree* by P.D. James and T.A. Critchley. Another
similar murder in the same district only twelve days later had tremendous
effect. This was the cluster of murders that De Quincey wrote about in his
essay 'Murder Considered as One of the Fine Arts'.

Loving Unsuitable People

All lovers love unsuitable people –
a Moslem loves a Jew,
a Protestant loves a Catholic,
and I'm in love with you!

A Capulet, from the whole of Verona,
will choose a Montague,
Housman loved Moses Jackson,
and I'm in love with you!

Noel Coward adored Jack Wilson
(straight as a ruler too),
and Don José loved Carmen –
and I'm in love with you!

Auden loved Chester Kallman,
Adam loved You-Know-Who,
Bohemians all loved Mimi –
and I'm in love with you!

Some Saints loved God only
(a funny thing to do),
while Bonnie loved Clyde Barrow –
but I'm in love with you!

Ah! Tristan loved Isolde,
and Byron's head of the queue
was prim Teresa Guiccioli –
but I'm in love with you!

Frankie, they say, loved Johnnie,
and stuck to him like glue
till it came unstuck in a shoot-out!
But I still love you.

Millions loved Shirley Temple –
what sentimental goo! –

in love, I'm afraid, with a minor,
as I'm in love with you.

It's always unsuitable people
that seem the first of the few –
and that might be the reason
that I'm in love with you!

Perfect love is a phantom,
a dream that won't come true –
but lots of us are in love with love
and I'm in love with you!

The Premature Coronation

'AD 310 September. *Although Sapor was in the thirtieth year of
his long reign, he was still in the vigour of youth, as the date of his
accession by a very strange fatality, had preceded that of his birth.
The wife of Hormouz remained pregnant at the time of her husband's
death; and the uncertainty of the sex, as well as of the event, excited
the ambitious hopes of the house of Sassan. The apprehensions of civil
war were at length removed, by the positive assurance of the Magi that
the widow of Hormouz had conceived, and would safely produce, a son.
Obedient to the voice of superstition, the Persians prepared, without
delay, the ceremony of his coronation. A royal bed, on which the queen
lay in state, was exhibited in the midst of the palace; a diadem was
placed on the spot which might be supposed to conceal the future heir
of Artaxerxes, and the prostrate Satraps adored the majesty of their
invisible and insensible sovereign.'* – Edward Gibbon, The Decline
and Fall of the Roman Empire, *Chapter XVIII*

It's all in Gibbon. It is. The cruelties, the tortures, the battles.
Intrigues of the eunuchs, the lot! The heresies, martyrs,
    the wars
stirred up from time to time by invidious competitive bishops.
    Barbarian hairy campaigns, the luxury life of the East,
rampant theology too, the Arians and Athanasians,

the thick Praetorian Guard with Emperors made by
the sword!
Then as now cry Alas! for History's dismal agenda!
But you find little nuggets of gold, such as scholars enjoy with
their wine,
laced with the Latin and Greek, the rumours, the quite
anecdotal.
Gibbon's humour is dry, and it's that of a rational man;
the things that he didn't believe are recorded with admirable
balance.
See the story above. It's a smile, not a laugh, up his sleeve.

★   ★   ★

Surely he relished the scene! As the queen lies in state on a
day-bed,
there are psalms and musicians, perhaps; learnèd men, all the
sages and priests,
a solemn hullabaloo, in the rich coloured silks and the satins
(Constantine dyed his beard – in the East, where anything
goes –
in parti-coloured bright stripes, all the lords and ladies
were lustful),
and there at the centre, the queen – jewelled and perfumed
and fat –
veiled, I expect; with a crown; and her nails painted red
as a ruby.
Likewise her lips, is my guess. Her skin is a beautiful brown,
oiled and exciting and soft, a prominent jewel in her navel –
naked, I think, below this. For the ceremony's there to
be seen,
a cloud of witnesses round, and everything solemn and proper.
Incense and hymns. A High Priest intones with a world-
shaking bass,
some cymbals are struck, as he bends with the diadem over the
sexparts,
curled and crisp pubic hair, oiled and anointed with nard,
an odour of sanctity! He lays on the crown, an orgasm
of ritual climaxing there. And we have another Great King!

★   ★   ★

Long pipes, wine glasses with stems, the most they will do is to
   chuckle.
   They are the civilized men. Such stories are not for the mob.
Long coats, long waistcoats too. Long views are what History
   teaches.
   Long-headed men, and of them Edward Gibbon most fit to
   be loved
for his long-term attachment to truth, and the style that's so clear
   and Olympian.
   Rien n'est beau que le vrai. Rhetoricians, avaunt! (he implied).
Let all those born-again boys who fancy themselves as God's
   Sales Force
   look on this man who worked years, not valuing money,
   but Fame!

The first volume of Gibbon's *Decline and Fall* appeared in 1776. The last two
in 1788. Gibbon was born in Putney in 1737, and died in 1794.

The Peter Reading Poem

Rūmpĕtў̆ | - tūmtĭ̆ttў̆ | - tūm ‖ tĭ̆ttў̆ | tūm, tĭ̆ttў̆ | tūm, ŭkŭl | ēlĕ̆
   Rūmpĕtў̆- | tūm, hăngĭ̆ng | dōgs ‖ rūmpĕtў̆ | tūmtĭ̆ttў̆-
   | tūm.

Bāshĭ̆ng thĕ | bādgĕrs ăb | oūt ‖ tĭ̆ttў̆- | tŭm ăll thĕ | rāpĭsts ănd
   | yōbbŏs.
   Rūmtĭ̆ttў̆ | tūmtĭ̆ttў̆ | tūm ‖ gāngs ŏf ŭn | spēakăblĕ̆ | ȳobs.

Tēenāg | ĕrs rūm | tūm ‖ tĭ̆ttў̆ | tūm-tĭ̆ttў̆ | ħead-băshĭ̆ng
   | bābiĕs
   Tūm-tĭ̆ttў̆, | ūmtĭ̆ttў̆, | ūm ‖ hōmĭ̆noĭds, | ālĭ̆ĕns, | oĭcks.
   ˉ ˘ ˘ | ˉ ˘ ˘ | ˉ ‖ ˘ ˘ ˘ | ˉ ˘ ˘ | ˉ ˘ ˘ | ˉ ˘
   ˉ ˘ ˘ | ˉ ˘ ˘ | ˉ ‖ ˉ ˘ ˘ ˘ | ˉ ˘ ˘ | ˉ.

Beginning of a Ballad: At the Literary Party

It is an Ancient Poetess
And she stoppeth one of three.
Oh what, oh what, oh what, oh what
But yestreen did I see?
Could it have been a BAD REVIEW
That thou didst write of me?

The Rivals

*'You have W. W. Gibson over there I hear. Have you met him yet?
I hope he's not being the success he expected to be. De la Mare I hear
talks of nothing but America and is keen on going out again. He made
a lot of money I think and got a lot of adulation too I think. I suppose
Gibson might make some money, but I can't imagine anyone giving
him adulation – there's something so very small and mean about the
man. Davies I hear is mad with rage that de la Mare and Gibson have
been out and getting rich before he's had his "go" at the Americans,
and is planning to go and read his poems at 500 dollars a time. So
you'll get the whole brood of English poets out there before long.
All the ones not helping in the war that is, tho' Gibson has written
several "moving" poems from the trenches damn him.'* – Letter from
Helen Thomas (widow of Edward Thomas) to Robert Frost, 2
March 1917

Holt and hanger and hill,
Beacon and barton and byre,
Mill-race and river and rill
And charcoal-burner's fire!

All the sweet meadow flowers,
Bryony, Old Man's Balls,
Call them with Pan-like powers
Out of the milking-stalls!

Loosestrife, bladderwort, vetch,
Hazel and hay and holly –
Tiny hands they outstretch
Make them juvescent and jolly!

Georgian Poets all,
All of them up to their necks
In country matters – but small
Is ever their mention of Sex!

Nature is censored and tame –
Picturesque is the word –
A bull and an ox are the same
For this land–literate herd!

Money excites them a bit –
Like the inns and the pints of old ale –
As they write, as they dreamily sit.
There aren't many cheques in the mail,

So it isn't surprising at all
That a chance to cash in stirs them up
To an envy by no means small,
And the bitterness of Life's cup

Overflows. And they itch to be off
To a land where the readings are long,
Where the hearers don't fidget and cough
and the singer is paid for his song!

Show Ban for Peke Breeder's Contempt

(A McGonagall Sonnet based on a Guardian report, 4 June 1985)

A wee ban has been placed, by the Kennel Club General
    Committee,
on Mrs Barbara Lashmar, aged 63, of Redhill, Surrey,
because she 'discredited the canine world'. They showed
    no pity –
she's banned from all dog shows for ten years because in a flurry
of temper she told how Miss Adele Summers (who fled from the
    judging ring in tears
with her dog 'Modesty Permits') had slept with gay or
    stud judges.
She said Miss Summers' dog was an effing cripple, and (it
    appears)
she shouted out, without any winks or nudges:
'Anybody that gives that dog a ticket is an effing crook!'
Miss Summers was very embarrassed and asked if she had to stay.
Mrs Lashmar was calling the other breeders every name in
    the book.
She shouted loud: 'Good. You're an effing big-head anyway!'
as Miss Summers went. Major General Martin Sinall,
Kennel Club Secretary, added an afterthought:
'We regard ourselves as very much the gentle end of Sport.'

An Arundel Tomb Revisited

('Their supine stationary voyage')

When we lie in the bed like an Arundel tomb,
stretched out beside each other like those two others
in the famous poem, one takes the hand of the other
(though we are living, and we're not an Arundel tomb):

it's because I love you and you love me –
however you define love, which of course has degrees,
everything everywhere exists in different degrees.
And it's certainly certain that Time doesn't love me

or you or anyone that's born of a woman.
Our faces alter, we get vague with pre-senile dementia,
with hesitating steps towards genuine senile dementia,
where what is what and where is where escapes each man and
  woman.

So this bed, like the tomb, is a ship – as Larkin said –
sailing onward into time, but not to Eternity.
There will be a landfall long before Eternity,
in the hostile sea of Time – as Larkin said.

The War Song of Lewis Carroll

I saw my little son without his head,
I saw the tortured and I saw the dead –
'Why, this is most peculiar!' I said.

I saw the burns, I saw the festered feet
of refugees with nothing left to eat.
'It's a solution, but not very neat!'

was all that came into my mind to say.
I watched the TV bombing every day –
that's the best war, the television way.

I saw the Kurds sent back without their cocks,
their eyeballs in their hands, no feet, no socks –
I said: 'This isn't very orthodox!'

'All war reporting is a monstrous cod!'
cried some. Some left a lot to God.
It seemed to me, in logic, very odd!

'It's quite extreme!' I yelled, 'mathematics men
would not believe it! It's a crowing hen –
and only fit for Cambridge – frightful fen!'

A General said it was a turkey shoot.
The convoys were quite fried – the men, the loot.
'A Victory?' I said. 'The point is moot.'

And some divines said men made earth a Hell –
that made my Anglo-Saxon pride both pout and swell.
I can't deny, they did it very well.

Only the Long Bones

*'The head gardener happened to be there that day, and I told him
how my husband was first buried at Bawli Bazaar, then transferred
to Maungdaw and after that to Akyab and finally to Taukkyan. It
was distressing to think of these graves being disturbed so often. Very
patiently he explained the policy of the War Graves Commission
and of course I could well understand why. "But how was it possible?
What remains?" "Only the long bones, Madam, only the long
bones."'* – Gweno Lewis, wife of the poet Alun Lewis, dead in
Burma, 1944

Only the long bones, Madam, only the very long bones,
we skip the fingers and toes – but we do remember the ribs –
of Lewis and Morgan and Jones.
Knuckle-bones, useful for dibs,
are given to prep school boys.
They're not much use to his nibs!

Only the long bones, Madam, only the very long bones.
Necklaces (fingers and toes) – you could sell them in a bazaar –
anguish I hear in your tones . . .
does it matter *where* they are?
Since most of him is here,
and you have come so far!

Only the long bones, Madam, only the very long bones,
all of them labelled and packed – and the backbone counts as
   long
(I thought you'd like to know that).
Move and bury. It isn't wrong.
It's the way the War Graves work.
It's a game, like Bezique or Mah-Jongg!

'Entrance and Exit Wounds Are Silvered Clean'

– Robert Graves

And was there love? Who knows? There must have been.
Although hot love, like war, has gone away –
entrance and exit wounds are silvered clean.

Those girls wrong-ended, telescoped, are seen
as tiny figures on a distant day;
entrance and exit wounds are silvered clean.

They're like old movies on a pre-war screen,
gesturing in eternal black and white.
Entrance and exit wounds are silvered clean

and cause no pain – they're only scars, I mean,
tokens of love's once urgent active bite;
entrance and exit wounds are silvered clean.

Blake in England 1988

The teacups of the bourgeoisie
mean we never can be free.

The knives that terrify the streets
make God's heart miss several beats.

The Devil enters in his log
each badger baited by a dog.

In Hell rejoicing of the rats
is caused by those who ill-treat cats.

The black man sings his undersong;
his Purgatory is white, and long.

The poor who sleep in cardboard boxes
are less at home than urban foxes.

The weapons in the silos moan –
for all these things, we shall atone.

22 West Cromwell Road

(Cabaret Song)

In front of the house
there's a barricading hoarding
(and the windows are practically none) –
it's a piece of anti-vandal tatty-looking boarding;
and the roof that kept out
the rain and the sun,
its time is almost done.

Underneath that roof
was the starting of our marriage,
it was thirty-three years ago now –
marriage is a something that sophisticates disparage,
and no one would claim that
at all times, everyhow,
it should be a sacred cow . . .

but it was in that flat
(or a duplex you could call it)
that two kids passed their immature days,
so I'm sighing for that house and the fate that will befall it –
we were happy in the
small family ways;
it very seldom pays

to look back at the past
or get songlike sentimental
but I know that the ball-and-chain bash
won't much care for *us* or be sorrowful and gentle –
because a house is only,
and always only, CASH
and a kind of valued trash.

NOTE: The tune on which this is (very roughly) based is Kurt Weill's 'I
Am a Stranger Here Myself', from *One Touch of Venus*, his Broadway show
of 1943. The gentle/sentimental rhyme comes from Noel Coward ('Try to
Learn to Love').

American Presidents (Calypso Style)

When de New President go to de toilet he fin'
dat de Ol' President done left a load O' shit behin' –

it do sticky his fingers and with all his might
he curse de Ol' President for all dis shite!

He tink it a most low an' disgustin' caper,
and to clear it up he's gonna need loads o' paper!

Statements an' affidavits an' transcripts an' trials —
de paper dat's needed is miles and miles and miles!

He'd like to say 'What da muddaskunt you done, man?
You cause more trouble dan is right for one man!'

But de Ol' President, he's away for life
in a marble mansion wi' his wondrous wife!

He's asleep wi'a knowing little grin showin' on he face —
he won't never go back to dat White House place!

You won't get at him all de winter through,
he's a hibernatin' hedgehog — he don' heed *you*!

He don' mind if dem teevee preachers
has private lives wi' exceptional features!

He don' need no upper, he don' need no downer,
he jes' goes on sleepin' an' his hair gets browner!

What does he care if de world go wrong?
He's sleepin', a-singin' dat Ol' President Song!

New President, he worry sick, he where de volcano bubble.
Ol' President, he sleep tight — 'cos he ain't got no trouble!

January 1990

Sea Song

A big boy kneels at the edge of the sea,
A big balloon brandy there by his knee . . .
Whisper who dares! Credibility fails.
Kingsley Amis is singing to whales!

A Little Loyal Ode to the Queen Mother on her 90th Birthday

Elizabeth Bowes-Lyon! It is fit that we
should drink to you in a very large G and T!
Mainly because you've been around so long
but also because you thought *The Waste Land* by T. S. Eliot
was called *The Desert Song*!

Marty South's Letter to Edred Fitzpiers

(The Woodlanders, *end of Chapter XXXIV*)

Deer Mister Fitzpiers

A'm writen to thee now to tell thee
what may lie heavy on thy belly!

Yon hiair that Barber Percomb took
that wer *my* hiair, by t' Holy Book,
a zold it to'm, – an' all to deck
proud Mistress Charmond's hiead an' neck!

Zo what thou stroak'st in't hers but mine,
zo pirty, vrom a maid divine
it might a' come! A girt injustice
'tis now to me, vor wheer thy lust is
theer might a' been some love o' *me*!

Zigned: Marty South, o' low degree.

The Thomas Hardy Blues

Bring me all the accoutrements of a furze-cutter,
the billhook, the leggings, and the gloves!
I want to be a genuine Egdon Heath nutter,

right in the middle of the aristocrats,
the decayed aristocrats, the prosperous farmers and the tenants,
and all their frustrated loves . . .

I want, if I can't be a furze-cutter, to be a reddleman,
permanently stained by the sheep-marking vermilion –
I'm not clever, I don't ever want honour and glory, I don't want
    a medal, man;

I don't want to be a diamond merchant
or a rich dairyman, hot among the milkmaids,
I don't want to own Wessex or make a billion . . .

I want to be a quiet observer of all their cock-ups,
how it's always the innocent people like Tess
who end up most frequently in their lock-ups,

and how there are always coincidences and misunderstandings,
mistaken trysts, lovers in the wrong places at the right time,
more than any sensible person could ever imagine or guess!

The Tart of the Lower Sixth

What washing of willies!
What spurting of sperm!
Does anyone
Have so much fun
As me – by the end of the term!

What coaxing of condoms!
What rides to a fall!
The Head's fat wife
Would give her life
To have such a beautiful ball!

What prodding by prefects!
What twining of necks!
A *roman noir*!
The whole of the choir
Sings of me and of my oral sex!

I masturbate masters,
The Head's on my list,
I'm proud to say –
Today's his day,
It's his turn to be French-kissed!

Repining, repenting?
I don't shed a tear!
Because I know
I'll be a real pro
By the end of my schoolgirl career!

The Influence of D. H. Lawrence on the Language of Gardeners and Gamekeepers in the Thirties

O hear the dreadful C-word
that makes the lilies faint!
While F-words in the greenhouse,
they fairly strip the paint!

The intercourse invoked is
what turns the roses blue!
Varieties of loving
all quite unknown at Kew!

The lightest of the pinks – all
go deepest red with shame!
The things they've never thought of
are mentioned now by name!

And in the rides where pheasants
have never heard of sex
or pondered on the rabbits,
it makes them nervous wrecks!

The foxes and the badgers
go round with knowing looks –
their innocence has vanished
through sophisticated books!

Like Adam in the garden,
the time he fell for Eve,
a novel's altered everything
in a way you'd not believe!